This book presents the facts of human individuality—in clear non-technical language that a high school student can easily understand. It shows why future advances in psychology, medicine, politics, race relations, education, and religion must be based on recognition of the infinite variety that exists in the human family, rather than on a simple and dangerous concept of "the average man." Individual differences are so deeply rooted and all-pervasive that they influence every phase of every life.

The implications arising from the facts of individuality are constructive and in line with our best traditions. Readers who are deeply religious will perhaps be surprised at the support they receive from a leading scientist.

Books by Roger J. Williams

The Human Frontier
Free and Unequal
Biochemical Individuality
Nutrition In a Nutshell
You Are Extraordinary

You Are Extraordinary

You Are Extra- ordinary

by Roger J. Williams

Random House
New York

The illustrations on pp. 14, 17, 19, 23, 24, 25, 29, and 30 are adapted from
Barry J. Anson's *Atlas of Human Anatomy*, 2nd edition (W. B. Saunders Co.,
1963).

The illustration on p. 26 is adapted from material presented by Marion W.
Maresh in "Paranasal Sinuses from Birth to Late Adolescence," *American
Journal of Diseases of Children*, July, 1940, Vol. 60, pp. 55–78.

The illustration on p. 39 is adapted from "Pain-Spot Densities in Human
Skin," by E. Charles Kunkle and George T. Tindall, in *Archives of Neurology
and Psychiatry*, June, 1957, Vol. 77, p. 605.

The illustration on p. 27 is taken from "Analysis of Breathing Problems," by
J. L. Caughey, Jr., *American Review of Tuberculosis*, December, 1943.

The illustrations on pp. 130 and 131 are adapted from *Nutrition in a Nutshell*, by Roger J. Williams. Copyright © 1962 by Roger J. Williams. Used by
permission of Doubleday & Company, Inc.

The quotation on p. 174 from Stuart Chase's *Guides to Straight Thinking*
(1956) is used by permission of author and Harper & Row, Publishers, Inc.

To Phyllis: whose charm,
good sense, love and
companionship mean
so much to me

Acknowledgments

This book has been a long time in the making and its contents have been influenced by a very large number of people whom I would like to thank individually if it were feasible. The members of my family are certainly included and my immediate associates in biochemistry at The University of Texas as well as many people from other departments of the University.

Actually, help has come from chemists, biologists, psychologists, philosophers, physicians, pharmacologists, physicists, anatomists, neurologists, mathematicians, economists and anthropologists from all over the world. Experts in government, criminology, law, history, business, education, speech and journalism have given me information or influenced my thinking—also nonacademic people: writers, publishers, editors, businessmen, ministers, priests and men in public life. All of these have learned something about the theme of this book. What I have distilled from their reactions and their vast expert knowledge has helped me make this book far more sound and sensible.

ix

Those who have touched the details of this book in the most places are my wife, to whom it is dedicated, the late Richard B. Pelton, Mr. James K. Page, and my three secretaries Miss Alice Timmerman, Mrs. Vida Griffith and Miss Dorothy Thiele, who have successively helped me with many drafts. If all this sounds as if it has been hard work, this is a bit misleading. It has been fun! One of the reasons for so many revisions was to get away from the labored quality of the earlier drafts and to get more pleasure and satisfaction out of the book—and into it.

There is one man who has helped so much in practical ways that I want to pay him a special tribute. He is Benjamin Clayton, president of the Clayton Foundation for Research, but who most of all is a shrewd, discerning and generous man. My earlier technical book *Biochemical Individuality* was dedicated to him. When I first became interested in the basic idea that lies behind this book, his insight took hold and he saw the benefit to humanity that could come out of it. On his own initiative without asking any expert advice he sent a contribution of $5,000 to further my efforts. That was twenty years ago. The initial contribution was itself helpful, but the encouragement and help that has come during the intervening years has been tremendous. It is remarkable that with a total of about five years of schooling, he could project the usefulness of my unconventional ideas when other much larger foundations and granting agencies with access to expert committees discouraged my efforts. Now as I get evidence every day that more and more alert, forward-looking experts are inclined to accept what seemed outlandish twenty years ago, I am especially happy to express my appreciation to Benjamin Clayton.

Contents

xii   Contents

Prefatory Notes

What are real people like? How do they get to be the way they are? Can we hope to understand our society without understanding the real people who make it up? Maybe in our attempts to deal with the problems of government and society, we are too much like tinkers who have barely heard of electricity, yet try to repair a complicated television set. Probably our lack of understanding of real people has a lot to do with the fact that we inhabitants of this earth continually cry out for peace, yet do not know *how* to attain it.

This book presents new information about real people; it is of universal applicability and reveals new insight into what we human beings are like and why society isn't as simple as *a b c*. It also outlines a strategy whereby we can learn to grasp our problems and those of our wives, husbands, children, neighbors and associates as well as those of a troubled humanity. No one who deals with real people (and who doesn't?) can afford to remain unaware of the material contained in this volume.

Socrates taught about twenty-four hundred years ago that to "know thyself" was paramount. In our modern day we tend to spend extraordinary sums to learn about everything else. Outer space, which is as far removed from ourselves as possible, is a favorite target. In the interest of balanced good sense and self-preservation, especially in view of the material presented in this book, this interest in everything besides ourselves should dampen. We should employ the tools of modern science *now,* to heed Socrates' teaching.

There are today among scientists many strong advocates of basic research. What can be more basic than understanding real people? A quest for such understanding cannot be narrow; it must involve many kinds of experts. Yet our society and our institutions are stacked against such efforts. Nowhere in the world are groups of people competent in human biology, including biochemistry, genetics and psychology, doing this basic research. Those who *talk* about such endeavors chronically miss the crucial ingredient in the recipe—as presented in this book—without which they cannot make the cake.

The idea of freedom has been rated by penetrating students of human philosophy as the number one "great idea" of all time. This book gives, for the first time, a comprehensive and conclusive picture of *why* this idea exists and why it is inevitable that it shall continue to be held in high regard by all men everywhere.

Albert Einstein is reverenced by a multitude of people today
—often from afar. He was noted for his intellect rather than
for his religious devotion; yet he said, "The cosmic religious
experience is the strongest and noblest driving force behind
scientific research." And again, "Science without religion is
lame, religion without science is blind." The writer presents
in this book a view of science that is not lame and a concept
of religion that is not blind—nor is it so diluted as to be
meaningless.

You Are Extraordinary

CHAPTER I

Dirty-
Gray
Man?

In our crowded world is civilization moving ahead toward the time when tombstones can be mass-produced on an assembly line—all bearing the same epitaph?

HERE LIE THE REMAINS OF A
NORMALIZED STATISTIC

In a statistical age will computers be improved, elaborated and refined so that in the end, instead of our writing programs for them, *they will write programs for us?*

These prospects do not sound alluring; "statistical man" has little to do with you or me or any other real person. But the blame should not be cast on statistics. Rightly used by experts who understand their limitations they are a boon to humanity. But in dealing with *people* they should be used *with care!*

Why? Because a group of people is something like a collection of colorful marbles. In the assortment of marbles all are reasonably round, but they are of different sizes; some are made of pottery, some of glass, some of agate, some of plastic and some of steel. They may be all colors of the rainbow, and individually they may be multicolored, striped, mottled, stippled, translucent, decorated with lustrous flecks and patterned in a multitude of ways.

Try to average these marbles and one comes out with nonsense. Marbles are not made partly of pottery, partly of glass, partly of plastic, partly of agate and partly of steel. Such marbles wouldn't hold together. Try to find the average color of the marbles; mount them on a circular disk, rotate rapidly and observe. The color comes back a dirty gray. But there isn't a dirty-gray marble in the lot! People are as distinctive as marbles, but when we attempt to average them we come up with dirty-gray "man." This doesn't have anything to do with you or me, for we are colorful, interesting specimens more marvelously unique than any marbles. Averaging when applied in this careless way to people can be vicious.

Do you want to fly from the world of conformity, designed for "average" people? Is our willingness to spend billions on space research based on the vague hope that somehow—some way—we can spread our wings and get away from it all?

Would you like to get away from yourself? What kind of person are you trying to get away from? Can psychologists analyze you and tell just how you will act? Can they by proper conditioning make you act the way *they* want? Do you rebel at the idea of taking pills to make you happy and pills to make you sober, even perhaps pills to make you buy and pills to make you sell?

Do you feel like seceding from the human race when you anticipate that when heredity is better understood, babies may be designed (using intricate blueprints) to be just what they need to be in order to play on the human team most effectively?

Humanity has on its hands a terrific population explosion problem. How about this for a solution? We could pass regulations penalizing parents by taking their lives away from them when they start overproducing babies. Farmers have become accustomed to receiving severe penalties for overproducing wheat. Could we become accustomed to even more severe penalties for overproducing babies? Aren't babies like wheat?

Or are they different? Do babies or people really matter? Statistics will work if the number of people is smaller or larger. Statistics will work without *you*.

This is what millions are thinking today: What good is an individual? What good am I? Our governmental system is based upon the rights of individuals and yet individuals seem to be evaporating before our eyes. Are we losing our privileges one by one, so that humanity can become a satisfactory statistical mass (or *mess*)?

If you are concerned about the real and lasting significance of individuals, if it all seems hopeless and you are pessimistic about the "inevitable trend" toward doing away with individuals, I have good news for you from the scientific front. There is now abundant evidence—I have assembled a conclusive assortment in this book—that on our arrival as newborn babies each of us brings along a host of highly distinctive inborn characteristics. This raises us to such a level that we as individuals cannot be averaged with other people. Inborn individuality is a highly significant factor in all our lives—as inescapable as the fact that we are human. Individuality can never be obliterated.

I first began to get a glimmer of interest in the question of what individuality really means when I had an ulcer operation years ago in Eugene, Oregon. It was my first year as a university teacher of chemistry at the University of Oregon. In the hospital after the operation I was given a shot of morphine to relieve my pain and put me to sleep. It abolished my pain but didn't put me to sleep. In fact it kept me wide awake and made my mind very active. To remedy the situation the doctor ordered a second and heavier shot. There was hell to pay. My mind speeded up with agonizing rapidity from one thought to another, second by second, all night long. And it was a long, long night full of torture.

Of course, after it was over I was thankful it was past, but being a scientist by inclination and training I was disposed to ask: Why did *I* react to morphine in this unusual way? The answer was not the kind that could be found in a book, hence it intrigued me more than it would have some others. I have always been inclined toward finding out about things that no one else has thought or written much about. I have never been one to go to the library and read exhaustively and thus come up with something interesting. My inclination is to evolve a question out of my own thinking and then go to the library and see if I can find any kind of answer. In this case I couldn't. Words sometimes cover up ignorance, and the word used to cover up this particular bit of ignorance was "idiosyncrasy." Reacting to morphine in this way was my *idiosyncrasy*. But to give a phenomenon a name doesn't explain it. This rather silly answer didn't satisfy me, but it was the only one I was to have for nearly twenty years—during which time the question lurked in the back of my mind and occasionally popped out at me. But I had many other things to do and think about.

I didn't realize at all—at the time—how important this question was nor where it would lead. I didn't suspect—at the time—that attempts to answer this question would lead to asking and answering many other questions, and that out of it all could ever evolve a book such as this one. If I had realized it then, I would undoubtedly have given more time and effort to trying to find an answer. This question was something like Tennyson's "flower in the crannied wall." If I could get the answer "all and in all," my knowledge of God and man would be greatly extended. It was only in later years, when certain laboratory observations confronted me, that I was brought back to the morphine problem and was led to ask again from time to time the question, "Why do some people react so differently to morphine?"

As if to give my interest a second prod, I experienced another "idiosyncrasy" during the same hospital stay. This helped me to realize—eventually—that idiosyncrasies might be widespread rather than extremely rare. I was next given scopolamine hydrobromide (twilight sleep), which relieved me of pain and induced sleep but also gave me some interesting hallucinations. It happened to be in a Catholic hospital that I had my surgery, and on the wall of my room was a picture of Christ talking to the "Rich Young Ruler." As I watched this picture I could plainly see Christ nudge the rich young man with his elbow (in not too dignified a way), as much as to say "Snap out of it," and I could see their lips move as they talked together. All this happened before the days of talking pictures and I observed no sound effects and was not enough of a lip reader to understand what they were saying. I was fully awake. I knew their lips were not really moving and that I was seeing things. Before I got through with this drug I had other waking illusions which I was able to talk about rationally even while they were in progress. I saw monkeys that were squirting streams of blood at me; later they were throwing soft mud balls at my face. They seldom missed in spite of my attempts to dodge. Even though

I knew perfectly well that there were no real mud balls and that there was nothing to dodge, this activity of the imaginary monkeys became very tiresome to me. But the monkeys enjoyed it! Another series of illusions was a most pleasant interlude. I had the illusion of cruising in a car alongside a beautiful seashore; I could clearly see the changing scenery, the cypress trees, the white sands, the clumps of grass, the brightly colored wild flowers, the blue ocean, the breaking waves. For a time it was a most beautiful experience, but it lasted too long and I was eventually fed up with seashore scenery. I wanted to leave the colored movie and retire from all activity and entertainment, but in spite of my being awake and rational all the time, I could not banish the illusions that forced themselves upon me.

Sometimes, though not always, people have such hallucinations when given "twilight sleep." Here was another example of an unexplained *idiosyncrasy*. Why do people react differently to "twilight sleep"? It was probably fortunate for me as a budding young chemist that I did not concentrate on the "why" of idiosyncrasies at this time. It would have been difficult to stimulate any interest in such research, procedure would have been difficult to map out, support for such "outlandish" investigations would not have existed and I probably would have had little to report to the scientific world.

During the next twenty years, besides helping rear a family, teaching my classes and guiding some graduate students, I wrote a textbook on organic chemistry which was used in three hundred colleges and universities and became a best seller in its class. During this interval my research efforts blossomed; I discovered and isolated a new vitamin, contributed to the knowledge of several other vitamins and made contributions to our knowledge of the biochemical unity of all living things. By this time my research and writing activities had established for me a reasonable scientific reputation.

During these years I encountered a few idiosyncrasies that piqued my interest, and eventually I became sufficiently interested in "biochemical individuality" and its implications to write a short article on the subject. Later this interest developed into a full-length book. Without attempting to drag readers through all my gropings, I can tell of one book that I consulted which brought home with complete conviction the idea that knowing about individuality is important. One of the students who came to me for advanced study already had an M.D. degree from Northwestern; he told me of the newly published *Atlas of Human Anatomy* by Dr. Barry Anson of that institution. Otherwise I might have remained in ignorance of it for some time.

This book was specialized, factual and technical but carried a real punch for me. Many normal anatomical variations were depicted and I was stimulated to find many others, so that after a time I became fully convinced that each of us is built in a *highly distinctive way* in every particular, and that *this is the basis of individuality*. Dr. Anson's book led me to realize—with the certainty that objective facts justify—that human bodies can't be averaged and that an adequate single picture of *the* human body, or any of its major parts, cannot be drawn. A picture which purports to show *the* human body is bound to be misleading and may be vicious in its effects. Later, in conversation, Dr. Anson told me that some so-called normal features of human anatomy that have received time-honored acceptance and have been copied from one anatomy book to another for generations do not apply to more than fifteen per cent of the population!

All of this information about individuality is good news because its far-reaching implications make sense; we are given a basis for realizing our own individual worth, and our high purposes are placed on a reasonable basis. It opens the door to a real and appreciative understanding of ourselves *and others* and of how people individually can make the most of the special equipment they have.

We often hear it piously said that people should be *"treated as individuals."* This is an empty and meaningless expression unless we know for sure that they *are* individuals and are acquainted specifically with many of the characteristics that make them so. Many supposed experts seem to take an opposite view; they think of people as manageable raw material to be molded psychologically to fit into society. If this view is sound, people are not individuals in any important sense, and there is no valid reason for treating them as if they were.

This book is based upon hard facts that no one will deny. Inherently they form the basis for revolutions in education, psychology, sociology, medicine and in all human relations. These revolutions are inevitable and may come more rapidly in this age of speed than we now expect. Particularly is this so because these facts will not lead us into embarrassment. Nothing that is good will be lost; everything that dignifies human beings and promotes their idealism will be strengthened.

These hard facts will bolster your morale if you think you should be "treated as an individual." They will convince you that you *are* an individual, through and through.

This does not by any means suggest anarchy. We do have to live with our fellows, and ways must be worked out for doing this. People are sometimes prone to accept and take for granted their own individuality, but are blind to the *individuality of others*—a blindness that cannot persist if we are to live together. We must use common sense and consideration in expressing our own individuality. If any one of us becomes too much intoxicated with his own individuality, it will be a good antidote for him to know that others possess a high degree of individuality, too. If each of us knows about the distinctive individuality of everyone else, this knowledge will serve to guard us against excessive egotistic individualism. This is something like the very practical expedient of fighting fire with fire.

This book presents for the first time conclusive evidence that you and I—also Tom, Dick and Harry, Ruth, Marge and Mary—*are* individuals. It also lets us see *why* we are individuals, and gives us a glimpse of the hundreds of ways in which our individuality bathes our entire lives. Treating people as individuals makes sense and takes on an entirely new meaning.

CHAPTER II

Outsides
and
Insides

It is well known that people
have distinctive fingerprints and that the natural perfume
which each of us carries is distinctive enough so that a blood-
hound can trail and identify us. These differences are trivial,
and especially if we stay out of the criminal class, are rarely
important. If we could look at the "insides" of our friends
and neighbors, however, we would be startled at the very
large internal variations—often much larger than we see
from the outside.

While these marked differences do not by any means
keep us from being brothers under the skin, they often have
a great deal to do with the details of our individual lives.
Many such differences are tremendously important and in
some circumstances can spell the difference between life and
death.

Stomachs, for example, vary in size, shape and contour
far more than do our noses or mouths. A person with a

stomach like Number I (page 14) would have a tremendous advantage in a pie-eating contest over one having a stomach like Number XII. All stomachs have some stretch to them, but the larger ones have more than the smaller!

The valvelike inlets and outlets to the stomachs vary greatly in size, shape and placement. They also vary in their operation: some stomachs empty rapidly into the intestine, some slowly. The upper (cardiac) valve operates so that some people vomit readily when their stomachs are upset; others almost never do. One of the world's greatest scientists told me that he was fully protected from ever becoming an alcoholic because even a little alcohol in his stomach caused him to reject it automatically by vomiting.

Is there uniformity in what goes on within our stomachs, regardless of their size or shape? Emphatically no. Digestion in the stomach takes place largely because of the enzyme *pepsin* which acts only in a medium containing a relatively high concentration of hydrochloric acid. A Mayo Foundation study of the gastric juices of about five thousand people who had no known stomach ailment showed that the juices varied at least a *thousandfold* in their pepsin content. Similar studies showed that the hydrochloric acid content varied similarly. A substantial percentage of normal people have no acid at all in their gastric juice. If normal facial features varied as much as gastric juices do, some of our noses would be about the size of navy beans while others would be the size of twenty-pound watermelons.

The positions of our stomachs also vary widely. Anson in his *Atlas of Human Anatomy* shows nine different positions of the stomach, ranging from being almost entirely up in the chest—from the breastbone up—to far down in the abdomen. Most of the nine positions are represented by five per cent or more of the population.

Differences in our stomachs and in their operation are

A "Textbook" Stomach

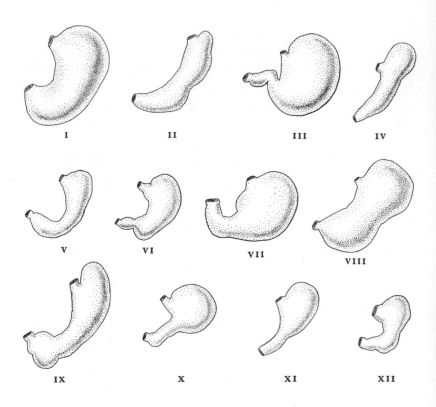

I II III IV

V VI VII VIII

IX X XI XII

Here are pictures of twelve *real* stomachs (after Anson) in contrast to the "textbook" stomach at the top of the page. These real stomachs neither look alike nor do they operate alike.

partly responsible for the fact that we tend not to eat with equal frequency or in equal amounts nor to choose the same foods. Attempts made by the Army, for example, to prepare a uniform balanced ration—containing in compact form everything young men are supposed to need in a day—have met with great resistance. A few soldiers may eat everything, but others will trade off or throw away what they don't want. Few are pleased with what is provided!

People eat with varying speeds. One of the factors involved in determining this is the size of the esophagus through which food must pass. I know by experience that my esophagus is large. When I was in college in Redlands, California, I never indulged in swallowing goldfish, but I remember demonstrating (in the orange grove which surrounded our college buildings) that I could swallow a section from a large navel orange. Some people have difficulty swallowing pills and capsules. These give me no trouble at all even if they are large. Physicians have different-sized "esophaguscopes" which they use for examinations. One of my former students had an esophagus so small that once when he got into difficulty he had to travel hundreds of miles to a city where an esophaguscope suitable for use with infants was available. It was found, eventually, that his esophagus was stopped up by a *small* grapefruit seed. It would take a sizable unshelled pecan to do this to me. People have accidentally swallowed whole sets of false teeth. This I think would be beyond my capacity. Anyone who has a large esophagus can, if he wishes, train to become a sword swallower; one who has a small esophagus had better train for something else.

One of the things we would see if we could observe the insides of normal people is very large differences in their hearts and circulatory systems. Pumping capacities of hearts can be tested externally, and it is found that the hearts of some healthy young men pump only three quarts a minute while others can pump about four times this much. The study of autopsy specimens shows why such variability exists. The inner construction of hearts does not by any means follow a single pattern. On page 17 are shown differences which occur in one part of the heart. Number I is an entire heart with its right auricle opened up to show how this part of the pump is constructed. The other pictures show how this same auricle looks in ten other typical hearts. These are far from duplicates of each other; in some cases they show little resemblance. In one of these (VIII) a small hole is present in the partition which separates the right and left auricles. This means leakage and inefficiency, but many people have lived to ripe old age with this or many other peculiarities in their heart construction. The insides of people's hearts—the valves, chambers, inlets and outlets—look much less alike than do the facial features of those who possess them.

In the picture of the entire heart you see outlines of the blood vessels that service the heart itself. These are by no means identical in different hearts. The left coronary artery is of particular interest because its stoppage is a common cause of a heart attack. This artery differs in size and in branching; sometimes there are two main branches, sometimes three, sometimes they are kinked and embedded in various ways. Of course, the stoppage of this artery is related to its size, branching and kinking, just as would be the case if there were a stopped sewer in your back yard.

I had a friend who although he seemed well, was athletic and took good care of himself, suddenly died recently of a heart attack at an early age. Evidently his heart had peculiarities that no one knew about. At the other extreme, a man may live to be so old, crotchety and irascible that many of his friends and relatives wish secretly that stoppage would

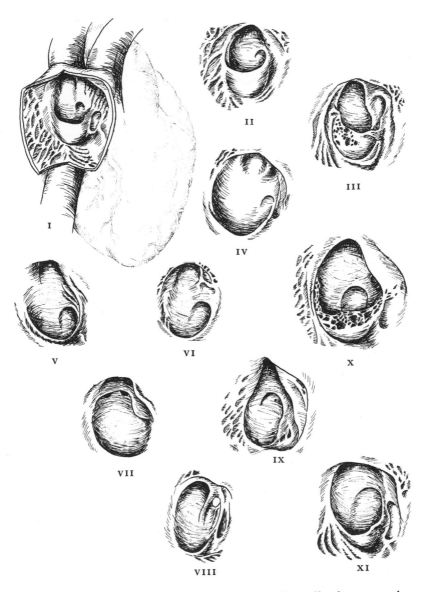

I

II

III

IV

V

VI

X

VII

IX

VIII

XI

This part (right auricle) of our hearts, as well as all other parts, is highly distinctive in construction, as shown in these pictures of eleven normal specimens. Hearts are also distinctive in their operation.

take place, but the blood continues to course through his arteries as easily as a summer breeze.

There are many inborn biochemical factors—too little explored—which also enter into the production of coronary attacks and the serious stoppage of blood vessels elsewhere, as in the brain, for example. Such metabolic differences may be far from trifling, as is suggested by the very large differences in the composition of the gastric juices of different "normal" people.

I had supposed, before I was introduced to Anson's book on human anatomy, that the piping system for carrying blood to all parts of the body was about the same in everyone. This is clearly untrue. On page 19 are shown some of the different ways blood takes off as it loops through the aorta above the heart. About 65 per cent of people have three branches something like Number I; about 27 per cent have two branches in a pattern similar to Number III. The other normal people, about sixteen million in our country, have *one, four, five* or *six* branches! Two examples of four-branch patterns are shown, but the others are not illustrated. It may be noted that the aortas and the branches coming off of them differ markedly in *size*. A blood vessel twice the diameter of another can carry about four times as much blood.

People who have more or less than five fingers or toes on each hand or foot are not considered normal, but "normality" in the number of branches coming off from the aorta may include anything from one to six! Furthermore, this variation in branching which we see in the aorta region can be observed *all over the body*.

The circulatory system is the one primarily concerned with the *logistics* of the body, *i.e.,* getting all the nourishment and the armies of oxygen-carrying red cells and the infection-fighting white cells to where they are needed, when

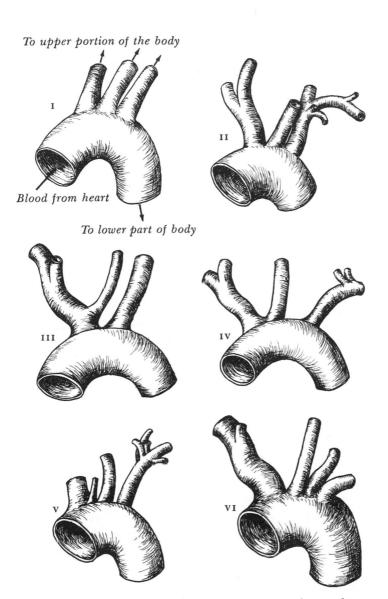

To upper portion of the body

I

Blood from heart

To lower part of body

II

III

IV

V

VI

These pictures show the branching of the arteries as they come from the heart. All these are "normal" but each is highly distinctive. The branching of your blood vessels and mine is distinctive, like this, *over our entire bodies.*

they are needed. Its importance in maintaining life and health cannot be exaggerated.

It would be childish to assume that every heart and every circulatory system always does a perfect job, that all through life every cell and tissue of the body of a "normal" person receives exactly the amount of blood it needs and that no organ or tissue ever gets an overabundance or is ever short-changed.

Temporary restriction of the blood supply to the brain causes fainting, and individuals, particularly past middle age, sometimes have chronically a too-limited supply of blood to the brain. This may be due to a heart of low pumping capacity or carotid arteries that are too small—or corroded on the inside with cholesterol deposits—or a combination of these and other logistic factors. Such individuals may lose their memories and other mental faculties many years before their bodies as a whole wear out. Others whose blood vessels to the brain are fully adequate may become physically weak and feeble as they age, and yet remain mentally alert up to the time of death. Things can be done surgically and otherwise to remedy such situations; just now, however, we are concerned only with the problems that exist.

A limited supply of blood to any part of the body can cause difficulties. If the brain lacks enough blood, it fails; if the blood supply to the heart is too limited, it fails; if the kidneys do not get all that they need, they fail. (There is evidence now that high blood pressure may arise as a secondary effect of the kidneys' not getting a full supply of blood.) If the sex organs get insufficient blood, they cannot function; if the logistic situation in the scalp is poor, hair won't grow and flourish; if the blood vessels supplying blood to the extremities are inadequate, one's hands or feet may be perennially cold.

This logistic situation can be upset temporarily when a

person who has limited blood supply to the heart eats a full meal. Blood is sent to the digestive tract to take care of its extra activities, and as a result the ever-working heart itself may be inadequately supplied, resulting in a mild or severe heart attack.

The importance of local blood supply is shown by the fact that when we bruise a foot or sprain an ankle or wrench our back, one of the most important things we can do to promote comfort and healing is to stimulate blood flow to the area by the use of hot pads or by soaking in hot water. The ordinary blood supply would bring eventual healing, but increasing the blood supply greatly speeds up the healing process.

Because of the unevenness of the blood supply to various organs and tissues, we are individually prone to have difficulties in those tissues and organs where the blood supply is least ample. But proneness does not mean that we will inevitably suffer. Medical scientists are extremely resourceful and many means may be used to obviate difficulties.

Even the blood that each of us circulates is itself unique. The blood groups A, B, AB and O have been known for decades. Many other "group" factors involving complex proteins in the blood are also known. The cell counts—the numbers of the different kinds of cells—are also somewhat distinctive. On page 22 are shown diagrams indicating that the chemical composition of blood is unique for every individual. Similar differences, which are far greater than the individual's external features, likewise carry over to saliva, urine, sweat, duodenal juice, stomach juice (already mentioned) and cerebrospinal fluid.

Marked variations in normal anatomy are found in other parts of the circulatory system and in the digestive tract *wherever we look for them.* Differences in the thoracic duct, in livers and in the pelvic colon are shown on pages 23, 24, 25.

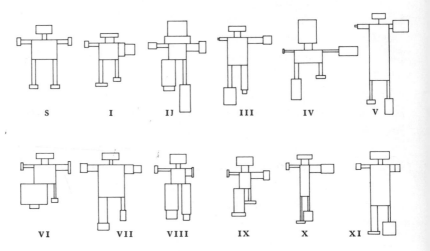

These are diagrammatic pictures showing the differences between the bloods of real individuals (I-IX) and the standard "textbook" blood, labeled "s." These ingenious diagrams were devised by Dr. W. Duane Brown, now a professor at the University of California, who analyzed successive samples from eleven healthy young men. Each of the eleven rectangles in each picture represents one chemical constituent of the blood. The longer dimension represents the average amount found, the shorter dimension represents the extent of the variation between different samples. The scales were so adjusted that the standard "textbook" blood was represented by a reasonably proportioned diagrammatic picture of a man. Each of the eleven bloods from the healthy young men was pictured using exactly the same scales, with the result that eleven *distorted* diagrams were obtained. No young man had blood like the standard; neither was any individual's blood like that of any other.

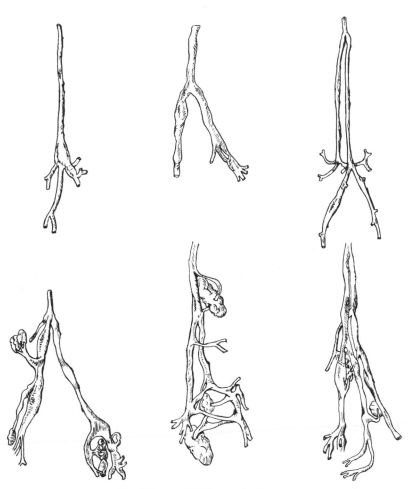

Six "Normal" Thoracic Ducts

The "thoracic duct" is the largest structure in what is called the lymphatic system. This system is responsible for picking up from the tissues a watery suspension (lymph) which travels sluggishly through lymph vessels to the thoracic duct and empties into the blood stream. Bacteria are like weeds growing in the body, and under ideal conditions these are picked up by the lymph and killed in the lymph glands along the way. Normal thoracic ducts, as may be seen in the pictures, vary greatly in form.

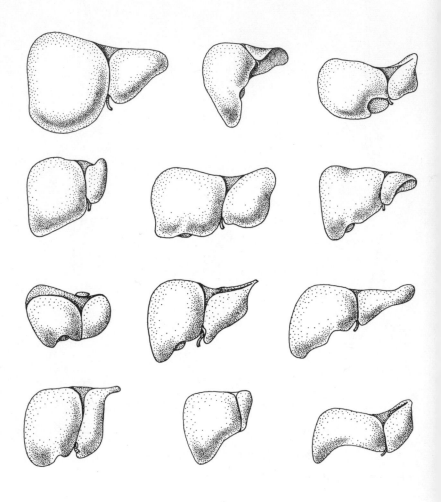

"Normal" Livers

In these specimens the total weights of the livers vary about four-fold. Liver size and efficiency may be an important factor in the complex problems of alcoholism, to be discussed later in this book.

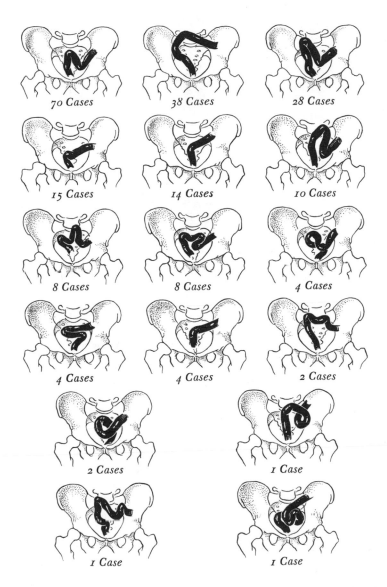

70 Cases

38 Cases

28 Cases

15 Cases

14 Cases

10 Cases

8 Cases

8 Cases

4 Cases

4 Cases

4 Cases

2 Cases

2 Cases

1 Case

1 Case

1 Case

How the large intestine (in black) is placed in the pelvic region in 210 cases is shown in these pictures (after Anson). Obviously, in the light of all that we have had to say about other bodily structures, uniformity of operation in this part of the body cannot be expected.

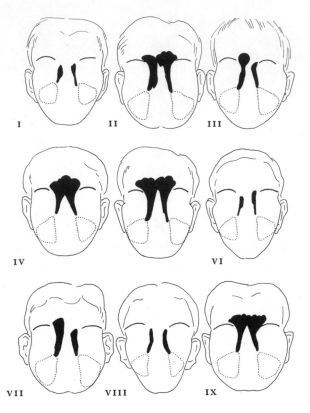

I   II   III

IV   VI

VII   VIII   IX

Frontal and Paranasal Sinuses in Nine "Normal" Children Ten Years of Age (From X-Ray Pictures)

These diagrams are adapted from studies in the Child Research Institute of Denver, Colorado. The position of the eyebrows is indicated by the curved lines. It may be noted that in Number I, for example, there are no sinuses above the eyebrow level whereas in Numbers v and ix these sinuses are voluminous. These pictures exemplify the fact that internal features of anatomy often vary much more than external features. The total volumes of the nine sinuses depicted must vary 20- to 30-fold while of course the children's noses, as we see them, would vary slightly by comparison. It is not surprising that children do not sneeze alike and that they are not equally prone to respiratory trouble and sinus infections.

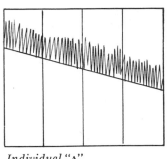

Individual "A"

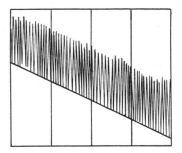

Individual "B"

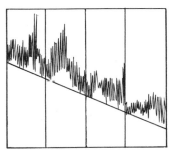

Individual "C"

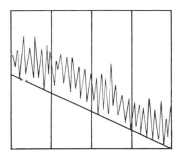

Individual "D"

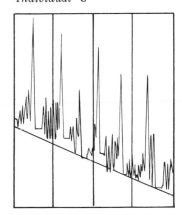

Individual "E"

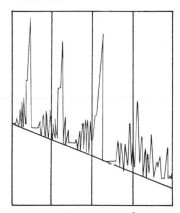

Individual "E" 2 years later

In and out breathing patterns (spirograms) of five individuals. It may be noted that these relaxed breathing patterns, which record the in and out movement of air, are almost like signatures. Individual "E" shows little change in two years.

That the breathing apparatus of normal people varies greatly is shown in the diagrams of the sinuses of nine normal children (page 26) and in the spirograms (in and out breathing patterns) of five individuals (page 27) .

Particularly interesting to some will be the normal variations in muscles. These make it possible for each of us to walk, run, talk, breathe, write, read, throw a ball, play golf or tennis or bowl in a way that no other person can quite duplicate. Variations in the *minor pectoralis* muscle are shown on page 29. Another place where variation has been studied is in the *palmaris longus* muscle in the forearm. This is one of the muscles involved when we flex our wrists. A total of about 22 per cent of people have peculiarities of structure or attachment with respect to this muscle. About 13 per cent of people don't have the muscle at all! An estimated one per cent have two muscles where there usually is only one.

The variations that are observed in hand muscles are of particular interest because even the most sedentary individuals make extensive use of these muscles. On page 30 are shown (in solid black to make them stand out) six typical arrangements of one specific muscle—the one which shortens when we point with our index finger. These muscles, like numerous others in our hands, are not placed alike or attached alike. The shortening of this muscle in hands I and V would pull on *two* tendons and would cause the index finger and the adjacent finger to straighten *together*.

One can find out something about the muscle attachments in his own hands by starting with the hand partly closed, then seeing if each finger can be straightened independent of the other fingers. If one can do this with each finger of each hand he has exceptional hands. In his case the extensor muscle for each finger must work independently, *not* like those in I and V. If one is sufficiently interested he can try the opposing experiment: start with the hand wide

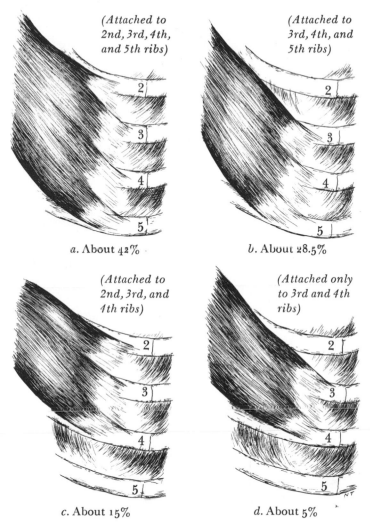

(Attached to 2nd, 3rd, 4th, and 5th ribs)

(Attached to 3rd, 4th, and 5th ribs)

a. About 42%

b. About 28.5%

(Attached to 2nd, 3rd, and 4th ribs)

(Attached only to 3rd and 4th ribs)

c. About 15%

d. About 5%

These pictures show how the so-called "minor pectoralis" muscle is attached to the ribs differently in different people. This muscle is involved when we draw our shoulders downward or forward. Each of us can do this, but each does it in a distinctive manner. Watch baseball pitchers and you will see that each one makes this and other motions in a characteristic way. Variation in muscle form and attachments is common in all parts of the body.

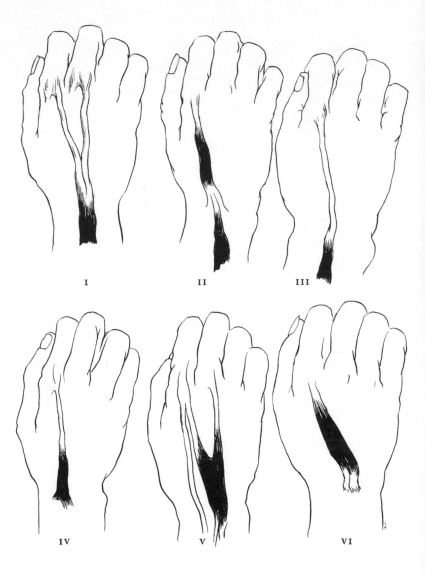

I   II   III

IV   V   VI

These illustrations show that the muscle (in black) which contracts
to straighten the index finger may have very different forms in
different "normal" hands. Sometimes, as in I and V, contracting
this muscle will inevitably cause the adjacent finger to straighten
also. Every hand is distinctive in its entire structure.

open and see if each finger can be closed independently. One will find, if he makes a test, that each person has hands that are distinctive in this regard.

It is no wonder that when we learn to write we produce our own distinctive handwriting, which has a legal status. If you buy and sign traveler's checks in your hometown, they can be cashed anywhere in the world by anyone who can duplicate your signature in the presence of the one who might cash them. This stumps even forgers, who may laboriously duplicate signatures but cannot dash them off in the presence of a cashier. Why? Because the forger has only his own hand, and everything that goes with it to make it operate; he doesn't have your hand with its distinctive muscles, tendons, bones and nerves.

Hand structure is of the utmost importance in connection with many everyday activities, especially if one is a pianist, violinist, typist, watchmaker, juggler, pickpocket, magician, baseball pitcher, football quarterback or even a masseur, osteopath or surgeon. We usually arrive at expertness in these fields by trial and error. A person whose fingers "are all thumbs" does not aspire to be an expert watchmaker or magician or to follow any occupation that demands skillful work with the hands.

Robert Schumann, the great composer, suffered severe and continued exasperation for years because he didn't know about these hand differences. He had strong musical leanings, composed music when he was seven years old, came from a good family and had access to the very best teachers. He also had motivation, determination and persistence, practicing seven hours a day. But he failed dismally in his highest ambition—to become the leading piano virtuoso of his time.

He had—for reasons which he did not know but we can easily guess—continual difficulty with some of the fingers of his right hand. He worked and worked on this and used all sorts of devices to overcome the difficulty; one was to suspend his fourth finger in a sling while he practiced with the others. Some reports are that he injured his hand—mutilated it—in his attempts to make it behave. It is possible that modern surgery could have relieved this embarrassing situation. He eventually gave up the idea of concert work entirely and devoted himself to composition. In this he made himself world-famous and probably contributed in a more enduring fashion than he would have if he had been merely a concert pianist. He lived in an age when recordings of performances could not be made.

One of my early students was an outstanding basketball player in spite of a small stature; he even rose to be mentioned as all-American. He was a premedical student and had a bad time with organic chemistry, which he took with me. He was a fine fellow personally and was willing to work hard. Eventually we pulled him through with a barely passing grade and he was admitted to medical school. (Today he wouldn't have had a chance of being admitted.) When he had finished his medical training he became a highly successful surgeon. As I reflect back now I realize in spite of my natural bias with respect to the importance of chemistry, that if I had to choose a surgeon, almost the first requisite would be a good muscular co-ordination and a skillful pair of hands. A good knowledge of organic chemistry would be pretty far down on the list of requirements.

An interesting case of hand differences has come to my attention recently—a quarterback on a football squad is a competent left-handed baseball pitcher but has to use his right hand for passing a football because reportedly the football doesn't "feel right" in his left hand. This is undoubtedly due to an anatomical peculiarity in his left hand which makes it difficult for him to open it up enough to grasp a football.

Some of the most far-reaching internal features that differ widely in normal individuals involve their endocrine glands —the *thyroids, parathyroids, adrenals, sex glands, pituitaries,* and the *pancreas.* These produce and release into the blood not less than twenty different hormones, each of which has a separate function. The release of these hormones has a great deal to do with our metabolic health, our appetites for food, drink, amusement and sex, our emotions, instincts and psychological well-being.

Each of the numerous hormones is produced by a particular type of cellular tissue located in a specific gland. A careful microscopic study reveals the fact that each individual has a differing capacity for producing each of these hormones. Thyroid tissue, for example, varies in weight in "normal" people from 8 to 50 grams. Parathyroid tissue in "normal" people is present in from 2 to 12 lobes and weighs from 50 to 300 milligrams. The "islets of Langerhans" in the pancreas, which produce insulin, vary in number in different "normal" pancreases from 200,000 to 2,500,000. The sex glands in "normal" males vary in weight from 10 to 45 grams. Sometimes undersexed (eunochoid) males have glands that weigh as little as ½ gram. The sex glands in "normal" females weigh from 2 to 10 grams. The number of primordial egg cells in the ovaries of a "normal" new-born baby girl vary thirteenfold.

Some of the endocrine glands produce several different hormones, so that a comparison of the gross weights of the entire glands means little. Our endocrine systems are unbelievably complex. Whenever direct measurements are possible, the output of each hormone is found to vary, among "normal" people, through at least a fivefold range.

Each of us has a complete endocrine system which is ours alone. We learn to live with this and adapt to it in a remarkable fashion. If we could be aware of the distinctive endocrine patterns of others, we would never be inclined to assume that all individuals have the same adaptations to make.

This is well illustrated in the area of sex. Kinsey's monumental works on sex may be criticized as to detail but they made one thing abundantly clear: among males and among females alike there are *enormous* differences in inclinations and activities. In men, the frequency with which semen is ejaculated (regardless of stimulus or circumstances) is one measure of sex activity. Kinsey in his study found one sound man for whom this occurred only once in thirty years. At the other extreme was a scholarly and skillful lawyer for whom it occurred more than 45,000 times in the same period. Matters of this sort are subject to exaggeration. That this instance does not represent a gross exaggeration was indicated a few years ago when the wife of one of our graduate students confided in some other wives that sex indulgence every night and morning was not objectionable but that she did resent repetition every noon.

Why people differ so enormously in this regard cannot be answered in detail or with certainty. It is obvious, however, that differences in our internal anatomy are involved to a marked degree. Not only are the sex glands themselves distinctive, but the adrenal glands which produce some hormones with sex activity are distinctive, also the pituitaries which produce a sex hormone which induces sex development.

Blood supply to the endocrine glands and to the sex organs is far from uniform in different individuals and is probably an important factor. In males, sex activity is made possible only when the sex organ is engorged with blood. Other things being equal (which they usually are not), a man with a high-capacity heart and favorably constructed arteries is more likely to be highly sexed.

I was amused to learn in Alexis Carrel's famous book *Man the Unknown* that he thought that sex activities are limited by intellectual activities. He indicated that a workman's wife can request the services of her husband every day, but artists, philosophers and intellectual workers cannot meet such a demand. I would be willing to wager that one's sexual appetite and capacity have virtually nothing to do with one's occupational, artistic or intellectual leanings. The examples of the extremely sexy lawyer and the able graduate student, as well as the facts we have presented about the individuality of our "insides," cast serious doubt on any such simple generalization as Carrel's.

We should certainly learn from the facts that we have presented, that no individual—man or woman—should be expected to behave with regard to sex as an "average" person. Each has his or her own built-in characteristics.

So far we have noted that normal individuals are highly distinctive with respect to their stomachs, esophagi, hearts, blood vessels, bloods, thoracic ducts, livers, pelvic colons, sinuses, breathing patterns, muscles and their system of endocrine glands. In all of these cases inborn differences are observed which are often far beyond what we see externally.

The most important way in which our "insides" show distinctiveness is, however, reserved for the next chapter, where we will be concerned with our thinking apparatus. It is in the area of thinking that human beings have their most distinctive gifts.

CHAPTER III

Bundles of Nerves

The "insides" of normal people include their entire nervous system, including the brain. We will find here also a high degree of inborn individuality —far more than we see externally. For our purposes we may consider the nervous system as having three parts: (1) the detectors or receptors; (2) the transmission system; (3) the interpreting and thinking apparatus.

We are equipped with nerve receptors which pick up sensations from the outside world, and sometimes from within our own bodies. These nerve receptors or nerve endings are of such great variety that no one knows just how many kinds there are and certainly not what each kind does. Twenty of the known kinds are pictured on page 37. Of these, some have fairly well defined functions: h, for example, is a taste bud which picks up taste sensations; j and k are in the retina

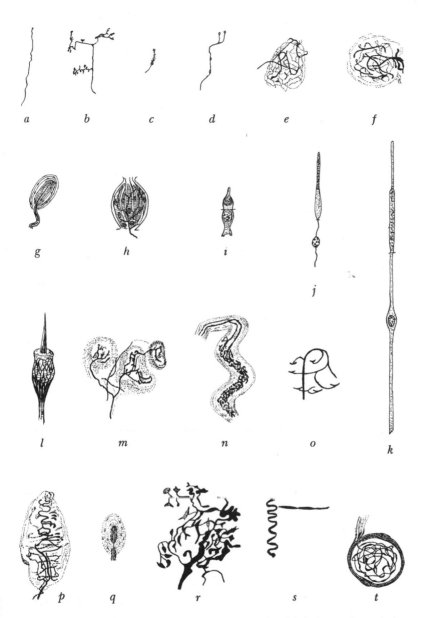

a   b   c   d   e   f

g   h   i   j

l   m   n   o   k

p   q   r   s   t

An assortment of nerve endings, many of which have functions that are as yet unknown.

and pick up visual sensations; *l* is in the ear and has to do with hearing. Many of these endings, however, have poorly defined or unknown functions which are open to speculation. The so-called Pacinian corpuscles (*g*) are characteristically present in the viscera of cats in large numbers and it is thought that these are "position sensitive" and send messages which make it possible for a cat to right itself promptly and land on its feet even when dropped upside down from a height of less than a foot.

On one's skin there are tiny areas which are sensitive to cold, other areas that are sensitive to warmth, still others sensitive to pain. These spots are sensitive because at these points are located appropriate nerve endings capable of picking up the particular sensation. All nerve endings are localized in this spotted manner. Next to a particular sensitive spot may be a blank (nonsensitive) spot, or it may be one that is sensitive in a different way.

A simple experiment shows that these spots are widely unequal in number and are distributed differently in individual people: Twenty-one pairs of normal hands were first stamped with ink, as shown on page 39. Then each marked spot was tested for its sensitivity to pain by pricking uniformly (mechanically) with a needle of uniform sharpness. The responses of each individual for each spot were recorded, as in the diagrams at the bottom of page 39. "No pain" was recorded as a *white square;* "slight pain" was recorded as a *dotted square;* "moderate pain" was indicated by a *hatched square;* and "sharp pain" was registered by a *black square.*

Each hand tested in this experiment showed uniqueness. The two diagrams on the bottom of page 39 represented two of the contrasting normal hands in the group. One hand had twenty-five spots that were insensitive to pain; the other had only one such spot. The first hand had no spots that were highly sensitive to pain; the second had nineteen such spots.

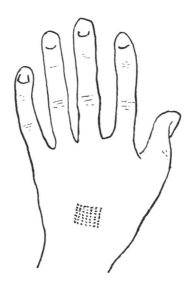

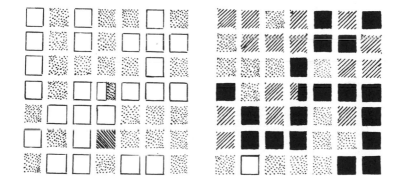

Pain spots on two normal but differing hands. Black spots are highly sensitive; white ones are completely insensitive. The others are intermediate.

People's hands (as well as other parts of their bodies) have always varied in their sensitivity to pain as well as to other stimuli. In the "good old days" women who were suspected of witchcraft were tested to see if their hands were sensitive to pain. If not, this proved that they were witches!

Similar observations have been made with respect to spots on the skin that are sensitive to cold and to warm. It is an inescapable fact that in the light of all we know that every individual is highly distinctive with respect to the numbers and distribution of nerve endings of all kinds—in eyes, ears, noses and mouths, as well as in all areas of the skin.

This has tremendous meaning because our nerve endings are our *only* source of information from the outside world. If the nerve endings are different in number and are distributed differently, this means that the information we get from the outside world is somewhat distinctive for each of us. How different and distinctive this information is can only be appreciated by a careful study of the special senses of "normal" people.

Differences in the presence and activity of pain receptors, for example, can make one "normal" person very different from another. An estimated fifteen per cent of people who have heart attacks have no warning pain whatever. At the other extreme there are those who have much warning pain even in the absence of any substantial heart damage. I know of one individual who had angina pains—sometimes severe—for at least twenty years; death came, however, at the age of eighty-six from difficulties arising outside the heart.

A study of the distribution of effective pain receptors reveals some interesting information. While we usually associate pain with damage, it is not unusual, in people who externally have ordinary pain sensitivity, for internal organs such as the kidney, liver or heart to be badly damaged by disease without there being any pain whatever. Severe pain may arise from the intestines when they are distended with gas, but there is no mechanism in them for picking up the kind of pain that might be caused by burning. Intestinal tissue can be burned severely (cauterized, for example) without giving any pain. No anesthetic is needed to nullify it; in spite of the damage there is no pain. In our brains, despite the abundance of nerve cells, there is no means for picking up pain sensations. Once the skull is open, the brain tissue can be manipulated without causing pain.

There are rare individuals who entirely lack effective pain receptors (this condition is called *pain asymbolia*). Cuts, bruises, even broken bones may cause no pain whatever. Curiously, in some of these cases some abdominal pain may be felt.

People who are *relatively* insensitive to external pain are common, and sometimes they engage in activities where this may appear to be an advantage. Ninety-seven prize fighters were tested in New York and eighty-seven of them were found to be relatively insensitive. The absence of pain in such cases, however, cannot be taken to mean absence of damage.

Since the types of nerve endings are numerous—and likewise the sensations they pick up—it would be tedious to do more than mention a few sample cases illustrating how individuality in this respect is manifest. Hearing, for example, involves specialized nerve endings. That these are not uniform in distribution and effectiveness in "normal" individuals is shown by studies of individual ears. When ears are tested for their ability to hear specific pitches, differences immediately show up.

In the first diagram (page 42) is pictured by radial lines the hearing acuity of the "textbook" ear, for vibration rates of from 250-6000 per second. The longer the line in the diagram, the greater the sensitivity. Following this first diagram is pictured in the same way the sensitiveness of eight

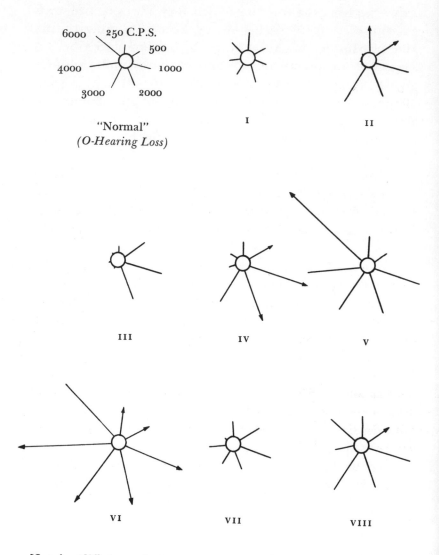

6000   250 C.P.S.

500

4000   1000

3000   2000

"Normal"
(*O-Hearing Loss*)

I

II

III

IV

V

VI

VII

VIII

Hearing differences in "normal" ears at different pitches are shown above. Long radial lines denote high sensitivity to the indicated pitch. Lack of such lines indicates deafness with respect to that particular vibration rate.

selected ears from Air Force personnel who had no recognized hearing deficiency. It will be noted that some ears are insensitive at certain frequencies and supersensitive at others. (An arrow at the end of a line indicates that the sensitivity was beyond anything measured.) One ear (VI) is supersensitive to all the vibrations tested. One can never be sure, unless careful tests are performed, how far his own ears are different from the "textbook" ear. Pitch sensitivity is only one aspect of hearing; the various differences which exist have a bearing not only on the question of whether or not noises bother us—and what kinds of noises—but also our ability to hear and appreciate music and to hear and understand words spoken in conversation or in movies, television or on the stage.

The nerve endings involved in seeing are complex and their functioning is highly complicated. Fortunately, in this area we are used to the concept of individuality. We know that "normal" people have distinctive eyes and that spectacles are not interchangeable.

People have striking individuality in two aspects of seeing which do not enter into ordinary eye testing. One has to do with seeing out of the corners of the eyes (peripheral vision). Because the rods and cones (nerve receptors) are not the same in number or equally distributed on the retina (and probably for other reasons), there are wide variations in "normal" people. In one test of a small group, the comparable peripheral-vision scores made by the individuals varied from 43 to 364. When a group of twenty-eight young men with 20/20 vision were tested for their ability to see peripherally the *movement* of a simulated airplane, one could see it move when the speed was two miles per hour, while at the other extreme, one could not see movement until it had reached a speed of ninety-one miles per hour.

Differences such as these play a large role in sports, in

driving cars or airplanes or in other activities where one's action must be timed with respect to what is happening in the visual environment. These and other differences which have an anatomical basis probably have a great influence not only on the ease with which individuals read, but also on their reading speed.

Another important phase of seeing that does not enter into common eye tests has to do with color vision. Of course, the simple red-green color blindness is often taken into account, but this is a minute part of the whole picture. Among those who have "normal" color vision, there are, because of the differences in numbers and the unequal distribution and effectiveness of the nerve receptors in the eye, many kinds and degrees of partial color blindness. Professor George Wald of Harvard in his extensive researches in the area of vision finds in some individuals unusual "richness" with regard to being able to see a particular color. Based on the extensive testing of Professor R. W. Pickford, a psychologist in England, it is evident that everyone has his individual strengths and weaknesses when it comes to being able to see fine shades of color. This means that we all have our own color vision and that what we see—in color—is not precisely the same as what someone else may see. There is room here for differences in opinion.

The nerve endings that pick up taste sensations in the mouth do not do the same job for all of us; "normal" people may respond very differently to such substances as sodium benzoate, mannose, phenylthiourea, sugar, hydrochloric acid and salt. In our noses the nerve endings are distinctive in their performance. We will have more to say about such matters later.

The late Professor Albert F. Blakeslee, prominent academician and investigator of Smith College, summed up much that we have been saying: "Different people live in different worlds so far as their sensory reactions are concerned." All of this has to do with *nerve endings*.

The second part of our nervous system is the communication or transmission system which for each of us is far more complicated than the telephone system of the entire world. Literally billions of cells are involved. Many of these cells are elongated in the form of tiny invisible threads, and like the wires in a telephone cable they may lie together side by side. These may make a visible nerve trunk. Nerve threads may or may not have a sheath or covering which is sometimes compared to the insulation around a copper wire. The resemblances to a telephone system are, however, superficial, since telephone (electrical) messages travel about 2.5 million times faster than nerve impulses and by an entirely different kind of mechanism.

If one is waiting for bumper-to-bumper traffic to move when the traffic light turns green a block away, he can readily appreciate that nerve impulses do not move with great speed. Even if everyone is attentive, each driver in turn, before he can move, has to get the visual all-clear message from the car ahead, send nerve impulses to the brain and have other nerve impulses travel to the foot that controls the gas pedal. The combined reaction times of the individual drivers may pile up so that the light is red again before one can move ahead a few car lengths.

Individual nerve cells in human beings may be a yard or more in length. In order to traverse a considerable distance a nerve impulse can, however, involve more than one nerve cell. At the synapses (junctions between nerve cells) there is no physical connection, but it is supposed that a chemical is released by one stimulated nerve which sets off a similar impulse—like an explosion wave—in the next cell. Impulses travel across synapses in only one direction.

To the best of our knowledge all nerve impulses are the same—equivalent to a "yes" (in contrast to a "no" when there is no impulse). In other words the impulse which travels does not say "cold," "warm," "pain," "light," "salty," "screetchy noise" or anything else; it is merely an impulse denoting the existence of a stimulus. There is usually an "all or none" law which eliminates the possibility that a single impulse can carry the idea of urgency. Either the "yes" gets through in full force or else it doesn't get through at all. Urgency may be indicated, however, by an increased number of impulses arriving from the same area. The possibility of making sense out of the impulses comes about by reason of the fact that our brain through its multitude of connections is able to discern in minute detail where the impulses arise and how many are coming. This brain mechanism does not always work perfectly. Sometimes, for example, messages from pain receptors coming to the brain are interpreted as coming from a different location than the actual origin. From the points of origin the brain generally knows, however, what the message is. Messages going from the brain to a muscle cell work similarly; they say merely "yes." In other words, "move," or more specifically, "contract."

The pattern of nerve branching all over the body is unique and distinctive for each of us, just as are the patterns of arteries and veins. Anson shows eight patterns of the branching of facial nerves. Each pattern applies to from 5 to 22 percent of the population. This branching is almost as diverse as the river systems on different continents and there is no set pattern that is followed or even approximated.

Such different placement of nerves may be of considerable consequence for the individuals concerned. For example, the sciatic nerve in the thigh is so situated and embedded in the tissues of some individuals that it is well protected against external damage. In others the pathway of the nerve is such that injury is very likely to occur in a fall or in an automobile accident, in which case the individual may be permanently crippled. In some individuals the recurrent laryngeal nerves (entering the larynx or voice box) are single and unbranched, and in others they may have anywhere from two to six branches. It is small wonder that our talk may be distinctive and not always with equal fluency.

Every organ and tissue in the body has a "telephone system"; how these organs and tissues function depends upon the messages they receive. Since the distribution of nerves (telephone lines) is distinctive in each of us, just as is the distribution of blood vessels, this contributes greatly to the diversity which exists within our bodies.

Finally we come to our physical brains located in and protected by our skulls. With its billions of cells, including many varieties (pages 130, 131), this is an incomprehensibly complicated organ. The naming of the various parts of the brain would introduce us to a number of technical terms without contributing materially to our knowledge of how it works. It is necessary, however, to answer the question whether the brains of all human beings are essentially alike physically.

The only writer to summarize our knowledge on the variability of "normal" human brains is the late Dr. K. S. Lashley, an outstanding investigator for many years in the area of brain and nerve functions. I will quote from him.

The status of the study of variation and inheritance of structure in the central nervous system may be summarized as follows. The brain is *extremely variable* in every character that has been subjected to measurement. Its diversities of structure within the species are of the same general character as are the differences between related species or even between orders of animals. . . . Discussions of heredity and environment have tended to regard the nervous system, if it is considered at all, as a vaguely remote organ, essentially similar in all individuals and largely molded by experience. Even the limited evidence at hand, however, shows that *individuals start life with brains differing enormously in structure;* unlike in number, size, and arrangement of neurons as well as in grosser features. The variations in cells and tracts must have functional significance. It is not conceivable that the inferior frontal convolutions of two brains would function in the same way or with equal effectiveness when one contains only half as many cells as the other; that two parietal association areas should be identical in function when the cells of one are mostly minute granules and of the other large pyramids; that the presence of Betz cells in the prefrontal region is without influence on behavior. Such differences are the rule in the limited material that we have studied. (Italics supplied)

Had he been writing for a popular audience, he might have added that brain cells and nerve cells in general are thought not to multiply after an infant's birth. This means that the nerve and brain cells with which we start life are the only ones we have to work with.

From the fact which Lashley emphasizes, that different human brains are as unlike each other as are the brains of different species and even different orders of animals, you may conclude that your brain probably differs from your neighbor's far more than your facial features vary from his. This leads us to the most important phase of individuality: *Each of us has a highly distinctive mind.*

While no one knows precisely how our brains work, we are all convinced that the brain has something to do with thinking, and it would be surprising indeed, in view of the differences in the structure of our brains, if it should develop to be a fact that we all think alike.

Even though our brains are distinctive at birth, they are all chock-full of ignorance. As we gain experience and have opportunities to learn, our storehouses of knowledge and insight increase so that when we become adults our stocks are highly distinctive both because of our spotted individual capacities to learn and of our varying learning opportunities.

It has recently been found in a conclusive, careful study that young rats that are sent to school (have all sorts of novel situations presented to them) increase the weight of the brain cortex (but not of the entire brain) by an average of about five per cent, compared with the brain cortices of rats that are kept away from the same learning opportunities. In this study there were no drop-outs recorded.

These increases in cortex weight were accompanied by marked biochemical changes but not by any increase in the number of nerve cells. The nerve cells individually increased their size and content. Similar weight increases in brain cortex could be induced by the same means in older rats, which is comforting. It is clear from these studies that our physical brains do not sit on the sidelines when we use our minds. Since our physical brains are highly diverse in structure, it follows that their development does not follow a stereotyped pattern.

Our individual learning experiences are not the same from the receiving end. As we have seen, the messages from the outside world even when we are presented with the same stimuli are by no means uniform. Our eyes, ears, taste buds and skin senses—in fact, all our means of gaining impressions of the outside world—are highly distinctive for each of us. The wide differences in brain structure contribute to make us all spotted with respect to the ease with which we grasp various thoughts, concepts and ideas. This is why we may speak of someone's having a "fine legal mind" or of a person's having a "yen for mathematics" or a student's being a "language whiz." Experts agree that every individual tends to have a pattern of mental abilities or potentialities which is distinctive for him or her alone.

Psychologists who are at the frontiers of investigating this sort of thing are convinced that our minds are exceedingly complicated. There are, so they say, forty or more facets to our minds, so that in effect there are at least forty ways we can be stupid and, correspondingly, forty ways we can be clever with our minds. Most of us are stupid and clever in a great variety of ways—all at the same time.

Some of the conspicuous ways in which people show their spotted intellectual capacities are in their abilities to learn mental arithmetic, to memorize numbers or names, to learn to spell, to think in terms of spatial relationships in three dimensions, to put words together skillfully to express ideas. I know of people who are exceptionally able in some of these ways and yet sorely deficient in others. For example, a person may be a whiz at mental arithmetic and yet be unable to learn how to spell at all well. Capablanca, who was well on the way to being a competent chess player the first time he played the game at the age of five, never distinguished himself in other ways. Some people have memorized the names and numbers in telephone books in the towns where they lived and yet couldn't do mental arithmetic or play chess. I have had students who were outstandingly able in most ways and yet were wholly unable to write up their ideas acceptably.

Some students have exceptionally good abilities with respect to all kinds of schoolwork—languages, mathematics, science—and yet have not had an ounce of creativeness as compared with many of those who had "inferior" abilities for day-to-day schoolwork.

Intelligence quotients (I.Q.'s) are convenient sometimes as a means of assessing a student's ability to do schoolwork. They are highly misleading, however, if they convey the idea that minds are patternless, and are all the same except for their degree of "sharpness." A person with an average I.Q. may be very sharp in some ways and quite dull in others. While he may be about average in several ways, his mind always has a distinctive pattern which becomes evident as soon as his mentality is scrutinized carefully.

What a person knows and what he can do intellectually are dependent upon his native endowment as well as upon the training he receives. These endowments are complex and many-sided and are capable of being cultivated to produce an enormous variation in the "finished product"—the individual's mind.

The basic answer to the question "Why are you an individual?" is that your body in every detail, including your entire nervous system and your brain (thinking apparatus), is highly distinctive. You are not built like anyone else. You owe some of your individuality to the fact that you have been influenced uniquely by your environment, which is not like anyone else's. But from all that may be known about basic inborn individuality—including a vast amount of material which we have not mentioned or discussed—it seems clear that the amount of individuality we would possess if we were all born with exactly the same detailed equipment would be puny, indeed, compared with the individuality we actually possess.

CHAPTER IV

Are We Really That Different?

In the previous chapters we have shown clearly and without question that each of us is biologically highly distinctive. Two questions come to mind: Does this carry over to practicalities? Even so, is this a matter of much concern in our modern day?

Biology too often involves learning a lot of names, and it is unfamiliar to many people. Can't this biological folderol be brushed aside; aren't we in reality all *homo sapiens*— about the same? Do people in their daily behavior, in their thinking, and in their attitudes toward a multitude of things, reflect the large inborn biological differences we have been talking about?

We can seek the answers to these questions with much more zest if we appreciate that *especially in our modern day* these questions and their answers are crucially important.

As the peoples of the earth continue to multiply, the "wide open spaces" tend to be replaced more and more by cities where crowding takes place. As an inescapable result of crowding, there is a need to organize people and to *regulate* them more and more. This means rules, and rules can cause conflict if people have strong individuality. Of course, if people are individuals only in a feeble way, the conflicts are correspondingly feeble.

In our society today we are engaged in making many rules, but rules are not a new development. Ever since the earliest human beings roamed the earth they have lived together for mutual protection, and freedom from rules has never been possible. Rules always make room for some conflict, because everyone wants—at least a little—to go his own way and follow his own leanings, breaking the rules when necessary.

Society always tends to say (in the interest of order, efficiency and harmony), "Do thus and so." Individuals tend to answer, perhaps ever so gently but sometimes vehemently, "Go to the devil." This is a fundamental, everlasting conflict —sometimes minor, sometimes major, but always present. It feeds upon crowding and upon a multiplicity of regulations.

Whenever society succeeds in formulating rules that are accepted by the people, common sense tells us that these rules simplify matters, contribute to efficiency and help prevent chaos whether they are set forth as laws or are merely customs. Society says that "all children should go to school"; "all people (except nudists) should wear clothing"; "all people should be vaccinated against smallpox." Such rules have been accepted; they are workable and have been so for generations. If society were to say "everyone must go to bed at night" or "everyone should go to church" or "everyone should wear a part in his hair," these rules or customs obviously would not be accepted or found workable because they conflict strongly with people's individuality.

It has been estimated that there are 23,000 kinds of jobs

in the world today besides many other activities which are recreational. In connection with the numerous changing occupations and activities, there are thousands of rules and customs which are being initiated and then experimented with continuously to find out by trial and error whether they will work. Some of these may cause untold friction and do great psychological damage before they are discarded as unworkable. The past is strewn with numerous customs which have been discarded and with hundreds of written laws that cannot be enforced. These customs and laws have failed not alone because of changing social conditions but also because in countless cases they were fundamentally not workable; they did not take individuality into account.

In a day when we are highly expert in the making of so many things, we need to become expert in the making of *rules*. These should be of high quality, ones that will not be disruptive or damaging. Unless we have a basic knowledge of what people are like, especially regarding their individuality, we are like workmen trying to be skilled carpenters without any perception of the characteristics of wood. We cannot hope to resolve, for example, the conflicts which currently break out between teen-agers and society, and between young people of college age and society, unless we know what the roots of the conflicts are. If individuality involves only trivialities, then we can cross it off the list of important factors, but if individuality is deep-seated, profound and far-reaching, we need to *know*.

Now as to the practical importance of biological individuality; it is a fact that "normal" people may respond very differently when they are treated in the *same* way. Furthermore, these differences show up even when they are tiny babies. About thirty years ago at the University of Wisconsin each one of a group of small babies was systematically stimulated in the same way by pinching a big toe, pulling the hair, holding the nose, being dropped from a height of four inches, and being exposed to a bright light a short distance away. It was found that the sucking pattern of each infant (which was being recorded mechanically) was changed in a highly individual manner by these different stimulations. This is in line with the biological fact that the nerve endings are not equal in numbers and efficiency in different individuals and the various messages each receives from the outside world are not the same.

In this same study remarkable differences were observed in the way different babies reacted to milk when it was offered at different temperatures. One baby in the group would not take milk if it was cooler than 73°F. nor warmer than 122°. One hardy little sucker, however, would regularly take milk anywhere in the range from ice-water temperature up to 149°F! I tried out putting my finger in water at 149°; this is 20° hotter than I can stand even for one minute; it is 45° hotter than what I regard a *hot* bath. The different babies varied greatly also in their reactions to different strengths of dilute salt solutions when they were offered in place of plain water. It is evident that the various nerve receptors differ markedly in efficiency from one baby to another.

At the Menninger Foundation a few years ago two investigators, a psychologist and a psychiatrist, found abundant evidence of distinctiveness in 128 babies that they observed carefully from four weeks to thirty-two weeks of age. Everything about them was observed—from diaper wetting and soiling, to feeding, sleeping, playing, crying and bathing. Some babies were found to be bold; others were shy; some reacted quickly to outside stimuli; some were slow. Some were aggressive and persistent when reaching for toys, etc.; others gave up easily. Some babies were very regular in their eating, sleeping or bowel-movement patterns; others were correspondingly irregular. Some could tolerate tensions and frustration readily; others couldn't take it. Marked personality differences showed up as early as they could be observed.

Dr. Wagner Bridger in New York recently made extensive studies of newborn babies, paying particular attention to how their heart rates were affected by all sorts of stimuli—loud noise, gentle rocking, a puff of air on the tummy, dipping a foot momentarily in ice water, being given a pacifier. Heart rates during sleep varied from 70 to 140 beats per minute for the individual babies, and were a sensitive indicator of the babies' feelings. A heart rate of 70 during sleep might rise to 140 during a crying spell, or one which registered 140 during sleep might rise to 220 during crying. Each infant presented a pattern all its own with respect to its heart rate and how the rate was affected by the different types of stimuli.

A series of twenty girl babies (all Caucasian) eight to thirty-six hours old was studied at Iowa recently. Not only did they show general neuromuscular differences, but with respect to vision characteristics, including eye movements and reactions, etc., their scores ranged with gradations all the way from ten (the highest possible) down to two and even one. Eighteen of the twenty scored below ten, yet all twenty had what is called "normal vision." That age and experience were not the determining factors was shown by the fact that the baby with the longest experience (thirty-six hours) had one of the poorest scores, while some of the youngest had high scores. These results underline the biological fact that in different individuals the numerous anatomical features of the eye, including the small muscles which control its activities, are by no means identical.

The development of a child into a distinctive personality depends to a large extent upon the uniqueness of his or her anatomy as well as upon the environment in which the bringing-up takes place. The rearing of children must be adjusted to the needs of each particular child. Each child needs to be treated as an individual because he is an individual. If he is treated otherwise, this is more likely to skew his personality than some inconsequential event such as the fact that the mother put him slantwise on the pot.

That individual children are innately different has for thousands of years been observed by parents having several children. Aristotle commented on this twenty-three centuries ago. We now know why no child can escape being somewhat distinctive.

The extent to which this distinctiveness is retained when we mature is remarkable. We may be sent to the same schools, we may wear similar clothes, speak similarly and follow many of the same customs, live in similar houses, have the same amusements offered us and have access to the same newspapers and books. But because the same messages do not come to us from the outside world, and because the interpretive apparatus of each of us is distinctive, we do not turn out to be uniform.

I found this out in a striking way several summers ago when I took the trouble to scrutinize a group of high school juniors who were brought to The University of Texas for an informal briefing. *Relatively* they were a uniform group— they were all about the same age, and in addition to being Texans, all were good students and interested in science.

Since the whole project was an informal one, I thought it would be interesting to play with them a game I had devised. I had made a list of fifty items, which included every harmless thing I could think of, that might legitimately capture the interest of a high school junior.

This diverse list, of which each student was given a mimeographed copy, is on pages 58-59. Each one was asked

1. Acting (in Shows and the Like)

2. Athletic Activities (Participation), All Kinds

3. Watching Athletic Contests

4. Beauty—Enjoying It As Seen Through the Eyes

5. Being a Leader in Some Activity

6. Betting on Contests, Races, Etc.

7. Buying or Selling, Bargaining, Dickering

8. Card Games of All Sorts

9. Carnival: Crowds, Roller Coaster, Etc.

10. Chess, Checkers and Similar Games

11. Citizenship—Being a Good Citizen

12. Collecting—Postage Stamps, or What-Have-You

13. Comic Books and Papers

14. Constructing, Planning

15. Conversation, All Kinds

16. Cooking, Preparing Food

17. Creative Work in Any Field (Art, Literature, Etc.)

18. Daily Routine Duties

19. Dancing—All Kinds

20. Dogs and Other Household Pets

21. Dressing Up—Making a Good Appearance

22. Eating, All Kinds

23. Fighting, Any Kind

24. Fishing, All Sorts

25. Flirtation

26. Gardening

27. Getting Haircuts, Shampoos, Massage, Etc.

28. Guns, Enjoyment of

29. Helping People Personally

30. Horses, Enjoyment of

31. Hunting, All Kinds

32. Inventing or Discovering New Things

33. Listening to Speeches

34. Loafing

35. Making Speeches

36. Marriage

37. Medical Care, Being Treated and Nursed

38. Membership in Clubs

39. Model Trains, Airplanes or Boats, Etc.

40. Music—Listening or Performing

41. Nature Study—Birds, Trees, Rocks, Etc.

42. Odors: Perfumes, Natural or Artificial

43. Ownership of Valuable Things

44. Photography—Taking or Looking at Pictures

45. Puzzles of All Kinds

46. Reading, All Kinds

47. Religious Worship

48. Riding or Driving Cars, Boats, Planes

49. Shows of All Kinds (Movies, Television, Stage)

50. Travel

to think of these items independently of anyone else and to register anonymously his or her reactions. There were twenty-two boys and four girls in the group.

Each was asked to consider the various items on the list as pieces of baggage which might be taken on a voyage to an imaginary heaven or Utopia where everything would exactly suit his or her individual tastes.

By means of successive selections, including finally imagining that their ship had encountered heavy seas and that in order to save anything one half to one third of their remaining baggage had to be dumped overboard, all the fifty items were, in effect, put by each player into one of five groups: (0) not wanted, (1) little importance, (2) moderately important, (3) important and (4) extremely important. The extremely important group of baggage items survived all the successive eliminations, and each was allowed to pass through the customs gate of Utopia after being given a rating of from four to ten depending on its relative value.

Unbelievable as it may seem, these supposedly uniform students with similar interests agreed on *absolutely nothing!* Every item on the list was placed in the "not wanted" column by at least one student; every item on the list was rated at least moderately important by someone of the group, and forty of the fifty items were placed in the "extremely important" list by some of the students.

Some few students liked (at least a little) almost all the items on the list; others chose to discard completely two thirds of them. Although all were following the same mimeographed directions (which allowed for latitude), some chose to take only three items through to Utopia while others took through as many as fifteen.

The various ratings of the item *Beauty,* as seen through the eyes, tells a story. There was one 0 (not wanted) rating;

seven 1 (little importance) ratings; one 2 (moderately important) rating; three 3 (important) ratings; the other fourteen gave extremely important ratings from 4 to 10. This is powerful testimony to the biological fact that in different individuals the sensory equipment (including nerve endings) is not the same and the interpretive apparatus is also highly distinctive. The possession of a distinctive color vision by each could be an important factor.

The item *Eating* tells the same story. The students were warned not to rate eating high because they were hungry at the time, but rather to rate it on the basis of its importance as a pleasure and satisfaction-giving item in their lives. Of the twenty-six students seven rated Eating 0; eight rated it 1; the other nineteen rated it higher—three rated it as "extremely important." The taste buds and the other sensory equipment are not the same in different individuals, nor is the interpretive apparatus. There is no fluke about these results; essentially the same wide diversity with respect to eating has been observed in a dozen similar groups. On this point, regardless of their bringing-up, people do not agree either as to what they like to eat or as to the importance of the pleasure of eating.

I belong to the group which gets only a moderate amount of pleasure out of eating; as far as appreciating my wife's cooking is concerned, this is a deficiency. It should be obvious that when I travel, for example, it is not primarily in search of the best restaurants. I am reminded, in contrast, of a relative, now deceased, who whenever he wrote a letter or postcard to us would, nine times out of ten, tell us what he had to eat wherever he had been. I suppose I could easily write a thousand personal letters or postcards and never once mention anything I had to eat. This relative lack of concentration on tasty food is not something of which I am proud. I do not regard myself as superior because of it nor do I regard my aforementioned relative as inferior. Such differences show that there is variety in people and in life.

There are those who regard being an epicure or gourmet (a pig with an ascot tie) as a sign of refinement and culture and sophistication. It is particularly a sign of really being somebody, in their eyes, if one is a connoisseur of fine wines! For personal reasons I regard this as hokum. I am biased— I am obviously not a gourmet nor a judge of fine wine. If I were, I would be more easily persuaded that there is something estimable about it. Something of the same bias makes me resist the idea that whether or not one is a he-man can be judged by his ability to contain quantities of liquor. My own personal container for such beverages is small.

Widely diverse attitudes toward *Reading,* all kinds, were shown in this game. This is particularly interesting because the subjects were all good students and it is often taken as axiomatic that a student is good or bad in proportion to how well he likes to read. It was not surprising that half the students took *Reading* all the way to Utopia with them, but it is indeed surprising that there were three even in this good-student group that rated it 0 (not wanted) and three more who rated it only 1 (little importance). There is no fluke in these results either. Again and again in different groups of students who showed excellence in science, essentially the same results have been observed.

How could there be uniformity when there are so many ways that eyes can differ anatomically and physiologically? Neuromuscular differences as well as important differences in the distribution patterns of rods and cones in the central region of the retina are probably important in making reading easy and pleasurable for some, and relatively difficult and taxing for others. I personally am one of those for whom the content of books is extremely attractive—if it were feasible

I would like to read on and on, but because of physiological limitations I cannot do so with enjoyment. More on this later.

If you are one of those who enjoy musical and theatrical productions of many kinds, you have my sympathetic understanding. I have a kind appreciation of Justice Oliver Wendell Holmes, who when chided about attending a burlesque show is reported to have said, "Thank God, I am a man of low taste." Because of *my* enjoyment of shows of many kinds, one of my pet expectations was that *Shows* of all kinds would certainly be rated at least moderately high by everyone. How far my own taste led me astray is indicated by the actual ratings. There were six among the twenty-six who rated *Shows* 0 (not wanted), and eight more gave *Shows* a rating of 1 (little importance)! We tend always to judge others by ourselves. Even Freud once said, "I always find it uncanny when I can't understand someone in terms of myself." I had this uncanny feeling when I saw the Utopia results on this item.

Conversation is another interesting item in that it was rated very highly (from 6 to 8) by seven individuals and 0 by six others. If you like conversation very much, you probably think everyone else does too, but this is not so. Women have the reputation of liking to talk more than men. This is probably so, but you can be sure that women are not all alike in this regard, and neither are men. Some boys and young men rate *Conversation* very high, and a series of nine promising high school girls which I happen to have listed separately from another playing of the Utopia game rated it all the way from 9 down to 0.

Conversation has a biological basis. It involves neuromuscular mechanisms of great complexity. Some children learn to talk fluently at an early age; some of us never learn the trick of it. This has always been true. Moses was a great law-giver but was "slow of speech and of a slow tongue" and had to enlist his brother Aaron as spokesman. It is easier for some people to learn to talk fluently than for others, for exactly the same reason that some can learn to run easier and faster than others.

There is not one of the fifty items in which the absence of inborn factors can be assumed. Certainly, for reasons based on detailed anatomy, these distinctive inborn factors play an important role in every item that involves sight, hearing, taste, smell and the sense of touch. Since differences in brain structure certainly have functional significance, we can say also that any activity which involves thinking has in it inborn biological factors.

As an experiment I suggest you take a pencil and play the Utopia game yourself. An easy way to do this without marring your book is to place a thin sheet of paper over the items (which are printed in **boldface** type) and then first mark with a 1 each wanted item. Go over the list again and again, giving additional marks to those items that merit it. Give up to ten marks if desired for some items.

After you have finished, see if your ratings are like any of those in the list on page 65, where for the sake of brevity there is a record of a random sample of half of the youngsters in the first group, indicating how they rated about half of the items. If your ratings agree approximately with anyone in this group, it is a sheer accident. Your ratings can't possibly agree with more than one of the group, because the individual members of the group do not agree with each other.

Many individuals in different walks of life have played this Utopia game, and always each player turns out to be a highly distinctive individual. A half-dozen groups of promising high school students have played it with results similar to those described. College students, males and females separately, have played it. Adult readers of the *Ladies Home*

RATINGS OF INDIVIDUALS (A-M)
ON SELECTED ITEMS

	A	B	C	D	E	F	G	H	I	J	K	L	M
Acting	6	7	2	2	0	0	0	2	0	1	0	0	1
Athletics	2	6	3	0	0	0	8	0	0	1	1	2	8
Beauty	6	8	3	8	2	1	10	8	5	1	6	6	5
Being a Leader	3	0	2	8	3	0	2	0	2	1	0	5	2
Citizenship	0	7	5	8	10	0	1	1	3	10	8	8	3
Constructing	0	0	2	1	8	7	1	1	0	2	3	0	0
Conversation	7	0	6	3	3	0	6	0	4	1	2	7	5
Cooking	3	0	0	1	8	0	0	0	0	1	1	1	0
Creative Work	9	2	9	2	2	0	1	3	3	2	3	2	1
Dressing Up	3	0	0	4	1	0	3	0	1	1	0	6	3
Eating	3	1	1	4	2	3	3	0	1	2	1	3	5
Fishing	0	3	1	8	0	7	8	0	0	0	2	1	0
Flirtation	2	0	3	3	0	2	10	0	0	0	0	4	2
Helping People Personally	0	3	2	1	9	0	0	0	6	0	1	10	1
Inventing	9	2	1	0	9	4	1	3	8	1	5	3	3
Loafing	1	1	1	2	0	0	8	0	1	1	0	3	1
Making Speeches	7	1	8	1	0	0	0	0	0	1	0	1	1
Marriage	5	2	9	8	9	0	0	10	9	8	9	9	4
Medical Care	3	3	1	0	3	0	0	0	0	0	0	3	4
Music	10	8	2	8	8	3	8	8	7	8	3	5	8
Nature	0	8	6	2	0	0	2	6	0	1	0	0	2
Reading	8	6	8	8	1	0	6	5	3	6	3	2	8
Religious Worship	1	10	9	10	10	10	0	6	10	10	8	10	3
Riding, Cars, etc.	5	2	1	3	3	0	2	7	1	2	0	7	7
Shows	8	4	2	3	0	0	2	1	1	2	0	8	6
Travel	4	6	1	1	3	0	3	2	2	3	0	2	7

Journal, staff members of the same magazine, Jewish college students, Protestant college students, Negro college students, American Indian college students—all have played it and have shown remarkable diversity within each group comparable to that shown by the initial group of students that I have described.

If we are trying by education and training to make people uniform, we are failing dismally. Every person continues to carry with him, as long as life lasts, a host of desires, tendencies and attitudes that are an outgrowth of his own inborn, highly distinctive make-up and unique development. Millions have been ruined psychologically because of a failure to recognize this fact.

It must not be supposed that each individual maintains the same set of rigid tastes throughout life. During development, maturity and senescence all kinds of bodily and psychological changes take place which influence how one would play the Utopia game. New experiences and contacts with new individuals may have highly significant effects. One never loses his basic individuality, however, and all changes take place within the confines of one's individual make-up.

How internal bodily change can cause one to change his or her tastes is illustrated by the changing attitudes of boys and girls toward each other as they go through different periods of sexual and emotional development. Also, as men age, for example, some may gradually lose interest in sex and cultivate other interests with a minimum of stress, while others continue to maintain a strong and perhaps futile urge. They can think of nothing more idyllic than living to be a hundred and then being executed for rape! Thus while no one remains static the changes themselves are distinctive, and no one ever ceases to be an individual and no two individuals' interests ever coincide.

As a device for getting people acquainted with each

other, playing the Utopia game has merit. I would suggest that any young couple contemplating marriage play it for each other and talk over the results so that they will not be blind to each other's peculiar characteristics. Certainly no two individuals should be expected to agree in their ratings, but they should have some things in common besides the desire to get married. Members of the same family could well play the game in order that they may understand each other better. Something is lost if the game is not played anonymously, but no amount of suggestion or pressure will make people uniform.

Nearly thirty years ago Hulsey Cason, a psychologist at Rochester, studied the *annoyances* of people in a manner somewhat similar to our playing of the Utopia game. He found that items that were *extremely annoying* to some people might be merely *annoying, slightly annoying* or even *completely innocuous* to others. Of course, as in the case of the likes of an individual, there is not complete consistency. Changes take place in individuals and what may be annoying at one time may not be at another, and vice versa.

Among the five hundred annoyances he listed, about forty-five had to do with hearing: among them the buzzing of flies and insects, howling of cats, barking of dogs, window-rattling, door-creaking, horn-blowing, chalk on a blackboard, sugar on the floor, radio static, noisy soup, shrill voices, nasal voices, rustling paper in a theater, eating popcorn, sniffling, whispering in church. How you feel about such annoyances will depend in part on the acuity of your hearing and the way your nervous system reacts to noises of different types and frequencies. Some people cannot even hear the high-pitched screeching of chalk on a blackboard, so of course they would not be annoyed by it.

I am among those who would rate many of these "noisy" annoyances high. I am sure that the hearing patterns of my ears have something to do with my being annoyed, but there are probably other factors. When a sudden noise (it doesn't have to be very loud) happens when I am relaxed and not expecting it, I can "feel it in my bones"; it actually *hurts*. When I am playing golf and about to make a shot, a noise at the wrong time can throw me off my timing. One of my golfing partners told me on one occasion that just as I was putting, he saw me shudder involuntarily the instant a cow in a neighboring field sounded forth. I missed the putt.

When I lived in Oregon I used to be awakened at daybreak—long before I wanted to get up—by song sparrows. I found a way to avoid this distraction. I simply turned over and slept on my right side; this made the birds shut up! This also works for crickets; they quit chirping or else chirp very gently when I sleep on my right side. A little investigation showed that I had an "island of deafness" in my left ear in the high-frequency range. My left ear was something like the one represented earlier (page 42, II). It was in this high-frequency range that the song sparrows sang and the crickets chirped, so with my right ear on the pillow their noises were inaudible or nearly so and did not bother me. Such islands of deafness are not at all uncommon, as the diagrams on page 42 suggest.

Cleanliness is something like "home" and "mother"; we are theoretically all for it. Actually, however, uncleanliness in its various forms is far more of an annoyance to some than to others. At least twenty-four items in Cason's list of major annoyances are related to uncleanliness of face, ears, feet, fingernails, teeth, clothing, bed and table linen, handkerchiefs, windows, floors, drinking glasses, washbasins and bathtubs. It is interesting that while some people may incline toward extreme cleanliness in all respects, others are inclined to be spotted in their attention to such matters. A house, for instance, may be the model of cleanliness in most respects, and yet cobwebs may be seen dangling from the ceiling by the ultra-observant. A person may be meticulous about the cleanliness of his person and yet wear dirty spectacles.

Biological factors enter conspicuously here. Unless people perceive uncleanliness, using their senses of sight, smell or feeling, they will certainly not be annoyed. Since the messages we get from the outside world are not all the same, we will not be annoyed equally by the same external phenomenon.

Because people's minds and senses are by no means carbon copies of each other, they react very differently, as Cason's study showed, to annoyances having to do with orderliness. Untidiness in dress, in one's room, in one's desk, in one's closet, on one's premises were rated extremely annoying by some but not noticed by others. Anyone who has had close contacts with different children knows that some become neat and tidy with very little coaching while others require much prodding and some are likely never to acquire habits of neatness.

For similar constitutional reasons involving, in part, differences in our internal timekeeping apparatus, waiting for an engagement, for a clerk in a store, for a telephone line to clear, for a green light or for a meal may be very annoying to some but of no consequence to others. Because people's minds are not identical, their sense of humor varies greatly. Jokes that are very funny for some are offensive for others. Some bring great offense, according to Cason, by "trying to be funny." One item found to be highly offensive to some but not to others was an adult talking "baby talk."

Some people tend toward the opinion that the truth was meant to be stretched a little and that white lies are appropriate and very useful. Yet petty lying was one of the annoyances on Cason's list which was rated high by some of his subjects. Some people look very lightly on cheating a little at a game—talking across the table in bridge or teeing up in the rough in golf. After all, they say, it's just a game. But on the other hand, these can be high-ranking annoyances to others who are meticulous about following rules. What may be an annoyance to one may not be to another.

Violation of privacy is high-level annoyance to some. They put high fences around their premises, pull down the shades and retreat into some inner sanctum even to write a letter or read a book. Others, on the contrary, tend to do everything in the open and may not pull down the shades even when they dress.

People are likely to be annoyed whenever their egos are rubbed the wrong way. Interest in ourselves is something we cannot expect to escape. The kind of self-centeredness which causes each individual to strive to maintain a good opinion of himself—honestly and intelligently—has much to recommend it. Whenever we do anything which reflects adversely on a person's opinion of himself, annoyance results.

There are a thousand ways in which one person can annoy another. Because our individual constitutions are so distinct and different, each of us reacts differently to every potential annoyance. If one wants to avoid being disagreeable and annoying to other people, it is essential that he become acquainted with and ponder over the numerous ways in which people may be offended. If one is dealing with a stranger, he can never know which possible annoyance may strike the stranger violently. If we want to avoid being annoyed ourselves, the best recipe that I know of includes the full realization that offenders differ greatly in what they regard as annoyances. What we individually may regard as the height of bad taste, and hence offensive, may in the mind of the offending individual be quite innocuous and harmless. Annoyances are most often perpetrated without the annoyer's having any intention of being offensive.

It is clear that the biological differences which we discussed in earlier chapters carry over often in full force from infants to young people and adults. Biological characteristics determine to a large degree the things we like and the things we dislike. As a consequence of crowding and of expanding activities, society needs to become expert in making rules and regulations which are not unnecessarily disruptive; this cannot be done without acquaintance with the individuality of the society members. Individuality is not a triviality.

CHAPTER V

Two Sides
of the
Coin

Will emphasis on the facts of individuality blind us to the truth that we human beings are members of one family and are bound together by a host of fundamental likenesses? Not at all. If we are to appreciate humanity we must know it as it is—its unity and its diversity. There are two sides to the coin—the *likenesses* side and the *differences* side, but it is the same coin. It is true that in this book we have been discussing differences, but this is done not to divide people but rather to bring them closer together. Paradoxically, we can realize and appreciate the true unity of mankind only when we recognize the tremendous diversity exhibited by individual members of the human family.

At a national meeting of scientists in Washington several years ago, when the relationship of science to public affairs was being discussed, I found lack of appreciation of the significance of human diversity all too evident. The presiding officer, then president of the American Association for the Advancement of Science, successfully quashed my attempts to bring a study of inborn human differences into consideration merely by saying something like this: "Dr. Williams is inclined to emphasize the differences among human beings; we will do better to think of their fundamental likenesses." It is probable that on this occasion I was not as adroit in my presentation as I should have been. It is also possible that my view was too one-sided. If so, my attitude has changed. I would now say, "Let's look carefully at *both* sides of the coin."

We human beings are all capable of reflective thought; we have invented and know how to use language and have a tremendous backlog of cultural heritage; we all have many of the same urges and appetites; we all enjoy beauty in some of its forms; we all have a moral sense; we yearn to be free— to be ourselves; we lean strongly toward religious worship; we are capable of altruism and even heroism; we are capable of love and aspiration; we are all alike in that we have human limitations, and paradoxically in the fact that each of us is different! If one were to say that people are so different from each other that they do not have affection for each other or do not need each other, he would be talking nonsense. It is abundantly clear that the differences that exist among people are not such as to prevent the development of powerful affection.

The idea that love and affection are based on likenesses alone needs to be corrected. Is a mother's love for her child based upon the child being *just like* the mother? Does a little boy's love of his dog depend on the dog being *just like* a little boy? It seems probable that love can reach its heights only when there are similarities *and differences.*

Superficially it would appear that concentrating wholly upon the fact that human beings are alike would be conducive to brotherhood. A more careful look shows, however, that too much concentration on likenesses and a neglect of the differences can wreck brotherhood.

In my family there were four brothers and one sister, all of whom have lived most amicably. Each of us has been consistently different from all the others. Two of the brothers went into the same line of work, but the specific problems which appealed to one often did not appeal to the other, and their individual approaches were highly distinctive.

I am glad that it was not drummed into each of us from infancy that all people are alike. If we had been successfully indoctrinated to accept this view, I would have judged my brothers and sister wholly in terms of their likeness to me, and each of them would have judged me in terms of my likeness to them. Disharmony would have resulted. Instead we all were taught more than usual, I believe, to respect each other's individuality. My mother was well aware of our differences. In my own case I remember that when as the youngest I sometimes became preoccupied with wandering about in the woods, watching the birds build their nests and rear their young, and was late for meals as a consequence, I got little chiding from her. She understood something about my peculiar interests and I suspect even knew that I didn't like food piping hot anyway. The differences exist whether we recognize them or not; an appreciation of their importance tends to build up mutual respect and to tie families together.

I know what my developing interest in the differences between people—now about twenty years in duration—has done for me. I confess that I have not always been a smooth-tempered, docile individual—always smiling and anxious to please. There was a time when I had enemies whose guts I hated. (Probably I thought of my emotions as righteous indignation.) Since I have become aware of the inborn differences between people, I like everyone much better and get along with a minimum of friction and a complete lack of enmity on my part. I have no enemies whatsoever. Knowledge of diversity has worked in favor of unity. While I cannot say with Will Rogers, "I never met a man I didn't like," I can say I haven't met one in twenty years I didn't like, and with my changed perspective I never met one I couldn't like now. Will Rogers must have known intuitively much that he did not learn from books or what he read in the newspapers! I wish I could live over certain portions of my life, knowing as I do now why all people do not tick alike.

Mutual knowledge about the differences side of the human coin can help greatly in the relationships between husbands and wives. When one knows about inborn individuality, little things take on an entirely new look. Henry N. Wieman, the theologian, has said, "Perhaps more lives are ruined through inability to deal with little everyday common things than for any other reason." Bruce Barton is quoted as saying, "When I consider the tremendous consequences of little things, a chance word, a tap on the shoulder, the dropping of a coin on a newspaper stand, I am tempted to think there are no little things."

Some of the "little things" that help tear people apart when they live in ignorance of inborn individuality involve distinctive reactions to temperature: coffee, food or soup may be too hot or not hot enough; rooms may be too hot or too cold or too stuffy; bed covering may be too warm, too light or too short; or it may be that beds are too hard or too soft; or the food too sweet or too salty or too spicy, or not sweet enough, salty enough or spicy enough. Sense of timing is often individual, and if one is silent, talkative or noisy at the wrong time, this can cause trouble; one person may be punctual and have a keen sense of time; to another, ten minutes may seem about the same as sixty minutes. If one is always too quick and the other too slow, this can cause distress. One may be too fidgety and antsy; another may be too serene and complacent. One may get sleepy at the wrong time or be "raring to go" at the wrong time. One may fail to remember and be continually losing things; another may remember things well that should be forgotten. One may be clumsy and awkward. One may be too well supplied with body odor and not bathe often enough; another may use offensive perfume. One may be naturally orderly; to another, being orderly may be difficult. One may be sensitive to the least jostling; another might not even know it existed. One may have little money sense; another may have too much money consciousness to get any pleasure out of it. (I remember reading an account of a European trip which had nothing to do with Europe; it was largely a chronicle of the various ways the traveler got gypped.) One person may speak indistinctly and wonder why he is not heard. One may hear well only when a single conversation is in progress; another may be able to get the gist of two or three conversations besides listening to the radio or playing bridge. Some individuals see just what is in front of their eyes; others have roving eyes and excellent peripheral vision, so that nothing in their vicinity escapes them. People are constitutionally different enough so that they cannot have the same tastes in music, art or literature and their attitudes toward different sports and recreations may be highly distinctive.

If one deals with other people on the assumption that everyone is potentially like everyone else, these very real differences are certain to cause serious trouble. Knowledge about the differences side of the human coin and an appreciation of how profound and deep-seated these differences can be, can only help to decrease friction and promote understanding between people.

Understanding of the facts of life, including the fact of

inborn individuality, can help greatly in the problem of race relations. Of course, there are biological differences between various races, but these differences are not as profound or far-reaching as the differences *within* each group. The tendency to judge people by their outward appearances (we cannot look at their insides!) leads us to false conclusions. We may look at Caucasians and conclude on the basis of their outward similarities that they are about alike. They aren't. We may look at red men, yellow men or black men and draw similar conclusions: all red men are alike, all yellow men are alike, all black men are alike. They aren't; a high degree of individuality exists within each group.

The avoidance of race hatred can be achieved only if we learn from childhood about the inborn differences between people and that they cannot be judged by outward appearances. If we *know*—this is fact not fiction—that members of a particular race show tremendous individuality, we cannot concentrate on hating that race. In order to hate a race we must have a single image upon which to center our hatred. Knowledge of the facts of individuality obliterates this image.

The truth has a way of setting people free, and we should have no fear of the whole truth. Poor racial understanding may prevail in spite of the superficial acceptance of the Pollyanna doctrine of human uniformity. It can hardly prevail if we have assimilated the facts about human individuality. Full knowledge of the truth will not lead us into trouble.

Anti-Semitism is an old disease, but it could not have reached its peak with Hitler and his followers if the German culture had been blessed with a knowledge of the facts of individuality. Jews were certainly not regarded as individuals who differed greatly from each other; if they had been so regarded, *really* and *deeply,* mass murders would never have been perpetrated. Wide recognition of the differences side of the coin would have helped tremendously in the cause of human brotherhood.

Racism involves the idea that there are superior and inferior races. This does not jibe at all with the truth. People individually have different patterns of potentialities; no person is generally inferior to another. A person who may be regarded as a half-wit may have a more serviceable stomach or liver than I have. Since every race is spotted with a great variety of individuals, each with a distinctive pattern of potentialities, how could we speak of a superior race? Superior for what? Mental abilities are always spotted, as we have made clear. There are many ways in which one can be sharp or dull, and each of us has a pattern all his own. Each race contains *individuals*, each of whom has his own distinctive characteristics.

Not only does a consideration of the two sides of the human coin help in promoting good relations with other members of the human family, including those of other races, it can do wonders in helping one appraise himself and keep peace with himself.

Joshua Liebman, a Jewish rabbi, wrote a notable best seller years ago in which he gave his well-substantiated opinion that a gift even greater than health, love, talent, power, riches and fame is *peace of mind*. By this I think he meant *inner peace* or possibly *peace of soul*, since the emotions are fully as much involved as the mind itself. He indicated that an important way toward the attainment of this "peace" is the "acceptance of ourselves for what we are—a combination of strengths and weaknesses." A person who imagines himself to be highly endowed may well consider that his responsibilities are equally high. One who appreciates, however, that he cannot jump across the Potomac River will readily be excused for not trying. One who has lesser endowments has also lesser responsibilities. Usually we have plenty of both—endowments and responsibilities. How much more peace of mind there would be in the world (and what a decrease in the use of tranquilizers!) if everyone could learn of his strengths early and with this insight accept the motto "Be yourself" as a valid basis on which to cultivate a life!

Pretense, affectation, sham and cheating often have their roots in the false supposition that one life should be judged by another. If it were generally recognized that every individual person is spotted with a multitude of strengths and weaknesses, people could more often be themselves and enjoy the inner peace which results from not trying to live a lie.

The vague idea that "almost anyone can do almost anything" can and has brought devastation to millions of lives. It has been said that in 1966 suicide was the number-two cause of death among college students, and it has been estimated on the basis of a recent study that for every one who takes his life there are ninety who threaten to do so. It is no wonder, in view of the social pressure which is put on so many to go through a prescribed academic mill when their aptitudes may lie in quite different directions. In a society in which this pressure is on, the vast majority of students must carry the stigma of being *failures* because only a tiny percentage can make Phi Beta Kappa. Young people often find that the idea of being a failure is more than they can stand. If they do not destroy themselves, they may become unhappy, frustrated and mentally ill for life.

This stress, strain and futility are unnecessary. The only failures are those who do not take advantage of their inborn capabilities. Young people need to think positively; this thinking needs to be directed toward the possible—not toward the impossible. How much of the mental disease in our country is caused by young people butting their heads against stone walls is not known. It is no wonder that students who have had a taste of freedom should be rebellious.

A healthy inner peace, however, does not militate against self-discipline, striving for accomplishment and overcoming difficulties; it makes way for the healthy ambitions and the natural aspirations that usually accompany general well-being. Most of us have more potentialities than we develop but some are stronger than others, and to be blind to our real shortcomings is unhealthy and can be devastating. A short-legged boy cannot win an Olympic medal for the hundred-meter dash, but there are other things he can do. A girl with a raspy voice cannot become a great concert singer but there are probably other things of equal value that she can do.

Recognizing handicaps is psychologically healthy. Helen Keller has said, "I thank God for my handicaps, for through them I have found myself, my work and my God." All of us should include our limitations as part of our endowment. It has been emphasized in recent years that "handicapped" individuals often are more dependable and have a better attitude toward their work than those whose bodies are perfectly whole and sound. All of us have—whether we realize it or not—this advantage of being handicapped. If we were fully aware of this, we might work harder, be more diligent and careful and thus bring more satisfaction to ourselves and to those for whom and with whom we work.

There are two sides of the human coin: the likenesses side and the differences side. Unity and diversity go hand in hand. This is a rule of nature. The more we know about both sides of this human coin the greater is our chance of living harmoniously with our families, with our neighbors, including those of other races, and with ourselves.

CHAPTER VI

We Are Little Gods

Before the facts of individuality can be accepted gracefully, there is one more hurdle to cross. If each of us has his own individual make-up and this influences the messages he receives from the outside world, if his distinctive interpretative apparatus influences his thoughts about these messages—the question arises: Are not our lives completely determined in every detail by the way we are built and the various environmental influences that impinge upon us?

Without minimizing the importance of this question, my answer to it is "No." This answer, however, requires some explanation, which can best be given by expanding our horizon and considering first what this world was like billions of years ago when, according to the geologic record, there was no semblance of life. In the poetic Biblical account "the earth was without form and void." According to concepts developed by my colleague, Dr. Robert Eakin, the first things related to life to appear on this planet were certain chemical substances—phosphoglyceric acid was a prominent one—which were able eventually because of ordinary chemical properties which they possessed (and still possess) to self-duplicate themselves in cooperation with other available chemicals. Eventually, because under the proper conditions some self-duplication took place, *accumulations* took place, and systems of self-duplicating and energy-using chemical aggregations developed after many millions of years. These aggregations did not possess life as we know it, but they became quite complex and had in their make-up many of the chemicals that we find today to be indispensable to life. This sort of thing went on and on for eons of time before such complex entities as nucleic acids (carriers of inheritance) came into existence.

Then there came a time when the first system originated which modern scientists would call life. Most interesting is the compelling indication that these most primitive living cells had in their make-up the very same minerals, the very same vitamins and the very same "left-handed" amino acids (about twenty of them) that are commonly found and used by living organisms today. These chemicals, some of which may be regarded as very modern discoveries, are actually billions of years old and have been used as a part of the mechanism of living things without a change of any kind during all the time since life began. These concepts, supported by a tremendous volume of sound evidence, suggest that if ever life is duplicated "in a test tube," as we say, it will have to be by an extremely long-drawn-out process and the resultant "life" will have to employ the same chemicals that have already been employed in eons past. There is possible, as far as we know, only *one fundamental kind* of life.

It is most remarkable to chemists, who recognize the potential existence of many millions of chemicals—each different from all others—that there should be such a "select few" used in living systems and such consistency of choice down through the eons of time. The evidence that this consistency has existed is so strong as to be inescapable. If this consistency were not a rule of nature, a mother robin feeding her nestlings a worm or insect would immediately kill her offspring, because a young robin cannot possibly tolerate in its food a selection including anything other than the *right* minerals, vitamins and amino acids. The young robin would die promptly, not only through failure to get a selection of the right chemical substances (baby robins must eat very often), but it would be poisoned if some wrong ones were included. Unity in nature is ever present.

Now that life was on its way, self-duplication continued. By now the process of self-duplication was complicated and had most of the elements in it that we find today when we study inheritance and genetics. Because, then as now, self-duplication is never perfect, variations (individuality) began to show and they have continued to show until after a billion years or more we have on earth an extraordinarily large assortment of very diverse living things. They seem extremely diverse in many ways—and yet, whatever their form, size or classification, whether microscopic in size or as large as a whale, they are made up of and use the very same minerals, the very same vitamins and the very same "L" amino acids in their metabolic machinery. This information is not more than about two decades old—to us—but it bespeaks a unity of nature and of living things that has existed since life began. Unity and diversity in nature have always existed side by side.

According to the poetic Biblical account of creation, God *spoke* into existence light, land and ocean, grass, herbs and living things. Since it is a poetic, figurative account it is not pertinent to inquire as to what specific language or dialect He spoke (there was no language then!). It is pertinent to inquire *how* He "spoke" in the figurative sense. In other words, what were the ways and means He used to bring about what came to pass?

Scientists have at long last begun to get a glimmer as to *how* God spoke life into existence. Certainly—with no intentions of being irreverent—He spoke with an extreme drawl —*very, very* slowly by our standards of time. But God is timeless and since we were not here yet, "time" by human standards was unknown.

To me, there have been three major steps of development of the biological world as we know it. *First,* there was the origin of life, about which we have already had something to say. *Second* was a tremendously significant step— the birth of some kind of intelligence and thinking. *Third* came the phenomenal beginning of free will, moral responsibility, sense of beauty and love.

Imagine what the world would be like if the first step had been omitted from the scheme of things. The world was once completely devoid of life. From the standpoint of our human way of thinking, it could easily have stayed that way on and on to eternity without one stir of life.

But it *didn't*. Life began. First the forms were simple in structure and had very limited potentialities. They simply vegetated. According to our human way of thinking, this situation could have continued on and on for billions of years with nothing phenomenally new making an appearance.

But this didn't happen. Somewhere along the line thinking and intelligence began to appear, we know not exactly where or how. This state of affairs, where thinking, inventing and devising were the supreme activities, might have continued on and on eternally.

But again, this didn't happen. Somewhere and somehow by means we cannot understand came the phenomenal birth of free will, of moral responsibility, of the sense of beauty and love.

As a scientist who tries to keep his eyes and mind open to all sorts of facts and factors that are in the world around us and impinge on human life, I see plainly the existence of three different kinds of things, or entities, all equally real and equally indispensable. First, there are *"material" things* like the molecules and aggregates of molecules that make up our bodies (and all bodies) as well as inanimate things—also energy, which according to modern physics belongs in the same category because matter can be changed into energy and vice versa. Second, there are *ideas,* which we have learned to hand down from generation to generation by books and otherwise, resulting in a social heritage from which we all may draw. Third, there are *aspirations,* a love of right as opposed to wrong, the love of beauty as opposed to ugliness, the love of fellow men, the love of God.

To me, ideas, music, aspirations, poetry, conscience and the love of beauty are all *facts* in the realm of human biology and are just as real as bones, flesh, proteins, enzymes and hormones or the energy from the sun. Anyone who is concerned with a well-rounded understanding of himself and his neighbors will take into account *all* these facts and factors.

Scientists (and I admire them and wish I were a better one) sometimes become overinflated with their own abilities to such an extent that they expect far too much from themselves. They sometimes expect to reason things out logically and find answers which human logic and reasoning cannot give. I am in favor of human minds' tackling anything or everything that they have a glimmering hope of fathoming, but this does not mean that I think human reasoning can be implicitly trusted, regardless of the conclusions it may deliver.

There are many fundamental questions that seem to be

beyond the capabilities of human minds. For example: "Does the universe have an end?"—"Was there a beginning, before which time didn't exist?"—"*Why* does every particle of matter in the universe attract every other particle (gravitation)?" Einstein made tremendous contributions to a more precise knowledge of how gravitation works but he never attempted an answer to the question: "*Why* does gravitation exist?" According to our human way of thinking, we might expect that particles of inanimate matter would have no affection whatever for each other nor the slightest desire to draw closer together, but they do, even when millions of miles apart! There are many other questions (some of them have developed in recent decades) which science cannot answer with an appearance of logic. One is: How can light be a wave motion (the propagation of which does not involve a corresponding transfer of particles) and at the same time be a stream of photons (particles)? Logically, it seems, it must be one *or* the other. But light is not one or the other; it cannot be studied in this modern day without accepting both of these antithetical ideas about it.

Many questions which impinge directly on human behavior belong in the category of those for which science and logic are not able to find answers. Why didn't the universe remain lifeless? Now we can make a partial answer to this on the basis of the discussion on page 82. We can say that it was "in the cards" for life to develop. Phosphoglyceric acid and other chemicals had the properties which made life inescapable—that is, after a long, long time. But there is another question: Why aren't the elements and their combinations so constructed that the world would have remained lifeless? (Pessimists might say that it would have saved a lot of trouble!) The best answer we know how to give is that this was not the Divine Plan. This is not a completely rational answer because we as humans do not comprehend the nature of things well enough to see how there could be a Divine Plan or how it could possibly have been formulated. We can use our intelligence enough, however, to arrive at the conclusion that some answers are beyond us—at least at our present state of development.

Another most interesting question: "Why did thinking originate at all?" This, too, we cannot answer except to say that it, too, was a part of the Divine Plan.

A real puzzler to those who think that human minds are capable of answering almost any question is this: "How can anything else besides heredity and environment influence our lives?" If these are the sum total, are not determinism and lack of free will inescapable? The logic of this reasoning seems clear-cut, but too much is presumed. Some scientists feel justified in denying the existence of free will on the basis that they are wholly unable to understand its workings.

Can we deny the existence of *life* on the basis of our inability to understand just how it arose? Can we deny that *thinking* takes place because we are unable to understand how people can think or how thinking originated? Obviously, such denials are ridiculous. It would be equally ridiculous to deny that people are able to take charge and direct their own lives because we do not see how this could be or how the ability to do so arose.

The acceptance of determinism is not compatible with life as we know it or with common sense. Some considerable number of scientists, including many psychologists, accept *in an academic way* (possibly only as a methodology) the principle of determinism, while at the same time denying its validity by every thought they have and every move or plan they make. One such scientist told me in these words, "I believe in determinism, but I always act as though I don't." The mere fact that he *believes* something implies a choice on his part and denies the principle of determinism. Another objection to this curious remark is this: what a man *says* he believes is relatively unimportant if it is in conflict with his behavior; he acts the way he *really* believes.

Incidentally, my definition of a scientist starts this way: "A scientist is a human being who . . ." A scientist is not an abstraction; no one of them should feel apologetic about his humanity. Scientists may love their families, enjoy poetry, music, art and religious worship. They do not have to step outside themselves to participate—not if they are, as I have suggested, human beings first.

The origin of intelligence is obscure. The existence of intelligence (which is as certain as anything) speaks for the existence of free will. Imagine that we are like chips of wood floating in the environmental ocean. We are tossed this way and that; we drift and bob about as determined by the winds, waves and currents. Water slowly seeps into us and makes us less and less able to float. Endow these chips with intelligence if you will; they are able to look at the stars; they can chart their movements; they can study the rate at which water seeps into their voids and determine how long it will be before they sink. But they can do nothing whatever about it! What a mockery intelligence would be without free will! *How* we can have free will is still a mystery, but we have it, as surely as we have intelligence. It, too, is a part of the Divine Plan.

There are many things about human behavior, such as reactions to specific stimuli, that we can understand and explain reasonably well when we have the underlying facts. But we do not understand how our brains work and how imagination, fantasy, poetry, conscience and love of beauty originated or how they work, so we are in no position to explain or account for all of human behavior. All of these unknowns enter into why we act the way we do.

My look at the total picture makes me think of human beings as little gods endowed with inscrutable but nonetheless real free wills and able to guide their own lives. We are *little* gods because we have limitations which we cannot surmount. We cannot run sixty miles an hour (our best sprinters make about twenty-two miles an hour for a short distance); we cannot will our hearts to stop beating; we cannot calculate with the speed of a computer. We are *little* gods because we can and do make mistakes; our freedom allows us this privilege, and demands that we accept the corresponding responsibility. We human beings have God-like potentialities because by using our minds, we can overcome many obstacles that may seem insurmountable.

Sometimes I have heard it said (and often it is implied), "If heredity is involved, we can do nothing about it." Of course we cannot individually choose our own ancestors, but the idea that we are completely baffled and impotent to overcome our hereditary limitations is ridiculous.

We human beings have, *because of our heredity,* little hair on our bodies to protect us from the cold. Are we doomed to sit and shiver when the cold wind blows? Not at all! We are little gods; we can wear clothing, build shelters, build fires, and take all sorts of measures to correct for this hereditary weakness. Many of us are born near-sighted, far-sighted or with other eye defects which make it impossible to see clearly and easily. Is there nothing we can do about it? Of course. We can wear spectacles!

For reasons of heredity we humans *see* radiation only within a narrow band of wave lengths. Insects, for example, can see light (ultraviolet) which is invisible to us. Is this hereditary limitation something about which we can do nothing? Clearly not. By photography and other means we can study, make visible and use not only ultraviolet light but an enormous spectrum of radiations that no animal has eyes to detect. Our eyes also have hereditary limitations, with respect to how far they can see and how small the object they can see. Are we therefore helpless? Not at all. We devise telescopes and microscopes. If we want to see action at a distance and around a corner—beyond the range determined by our hereditary eyesight—we invent television.

Because of heredity our ears are not as sharp as those of a dog, for example. Does this leave us frustrated? Not at all. We can study and utilize sounds far beyond the range that a dog can hear, and by the use of telephones we can correct for our hereditary inability to hear at great distances. We end up being incomparably more capable, earwise, than dogs.

We human beings began very early to correct for our hereditary deficiencies. When early members of the human race wanted to move a rock which required more strength than heredity had given them, they invented a lever which made such movement possible. Early men found they were not (by heredity) very good load-carriers; they did not have the strength of an elephant or the endurance of a donkey, so they overcame the hereditary physical weakness by domesticating these animals to do things for them. They also invented the wheel, which greatly increased their capacity to do things.

Human beings are *masterful* when it comes to conquering the limitations imposed by heredity and they will continue to progress in this regard. In recent centuries we have overcome our natural limitations in the spread of culture. Only a limited number of manuscripts could be written, so we invented printing presses. Paintings, for example, once they were produced could only be seen by a limited few, so we learned how to make beautiful reproductions. Musical productions were once largely lost the moment the performance was over, because the ability to remember was limited by heredity. We have learned to preserve such performances with extreme fidelity, and thus overcame the weakness of leaky memories. By heredity we cannot perform complex mental arithmetic, so we learned first to write, and later we have learned to build calculating machines that can far out-strip our human limitations. We have invented means of travel which make it possible for us to range far and wide and overcome our hereditary restriction of not being able to walk or run very fast or very far. Leonardo da Vinci was one of the first who sought to overcome the hereditary weakness imposed on us by our not being able to fly like birds. After centuries we have learned, so now we fly incomparably faster and farther than any bird.

We have done wonders in the field of medicine to over-come our inherited susceptibilities to disease caused by our ever-present bacterial and other enemies. As long as we did nothing to cope with this weakness, our life expectancy was about half what it is now. Only recently have we learned how to correct by surgery inadequate blood vessels which we received by inheritance, or even hearts in which because of heredity there is malformation, leakage or valves that do not work properly.

In future times we will learn how to prevent many of the illnesses to which by heredity we are prone. Deformed and mentally defective babies—who are extraordinarily handicapped by their heredity—need not continue to be pro-duced when we become more expert in learning the facts of heredity and all the intricacies of prenatal care and nutri-tion, as they are influenced by the individuality which is the possession of all.

As little gods capable of using our minds we should take full advantage of our opportunities. Sometimes there has been a tendency to shackle and strait-jacket our minds by formulating *rules* to think by. Sometimes these rules are formalized and called "the scientific method." In view of the individuality of people's minds and the freedom we possess, such rules may be an abomination. I agree with Percy Bridgman, the Nobel Prize winner, who said, "There is no scientific method as such, but the vital feature of the scientist's procedure has been to do the utmost with his mind, *no holds barred.*"

Each of us is born with distinctive equipment—more equipment than we learn to use. Each of us has the responsibility of living his own life, and making the best use of the equipment he has. Everyone can accept as a challenge his own individuality and the freedom with which he is endowed. With what we have, how can we do the most?

CHAPTER VII

A New and Different World

Those who for decades have been thinking exclusively within the framework of a world made up mostly of "normal" people will have difficulty changing their perspective to think of a world made up of individuals, each with highly distinctive inborn characteristics that influence every day and every minute of each life.

There is no facet of human life that is not altered by such a change of view; every kind of human activity and every study of human activity past or present will need to be reexamined in the light of the far-reaching facts of individuality as we now know them. Many books of many different kinds will have to be rewritten because they have left out or minimized the role of individuality. These changes in outlook will certainly come when the facts of individuality are accepted, digested and incorporated into our everyday thinking.

The interaction between human minds is subject to new interpretation. We are accustomed to think that if two "normally intelligent" people disagree, it is either because their self-interest clouds their thinking or because of differences in their respective rearing—they have been brought up differently and harbor the accumulated opinions and attitudes to which they have been exposed. These are two important reasons for disagreement. However, there is a third reason—sometimes even more important—that the facts of human individuality reveal: people's minds are inherently distinctive. Since their sensory apparatus and their interpretive apparatus is unique; they cannot consistently come up with the same answers. Children raised in the same environment sometimes violently disagree on many subjects where self-interest is not involved. Sometimes people cannot agree, even if they try. In general, two people can never agree *on everything*—not if each one is thinking for himself or herself.

Let us think, for example, how our minds react to the statements listed below. These are chosen with the idea that everyone (except Marxists) will probably agree that each statement contains some element of truth.

> Individual rights are the cornerstone of a successful
>   society.
> Freedom entails responsibility.
> The rights of minorities should be respected.
> You have the poor always with you.
> Backward parts of our country need to advance to a
>   higher level.
> More affluent individuals should help the less fortunate.
> Frugality helps prevent want.
> Wealthy countries should help backward ones.
> If any would not work, neither should he eat.

Each one of us will come up with a distinctive assortment of reactions to these statements. We will each want to emphasize, modify or qualify the various statements in our own particular way.

First we run into the problem of words. The individual statements do not mean the same thing to different people nor is their meaning usually simple and unchangeable. Webster's dictionary uses 235 lines to explain the meaning of the word "the." Most of the words in the above statements are more complicated than "the" and carry many meanings to many people partly because of differences in the patterns of their minds. Next, our individual make-up will help determine our attitude toward the sentiment expressed by each of the statements. If one has always had reasonably satisfactory relationships with parents, teachers, employers, he may give tolerant assent to the first statement, but he will not feel very keenly on the subject. If, however, one is inclined to have somewhat bizarre tastes, if one is critical of schools, business and politics, and is by nature a nonconformist, he may look upon this statement about individual rights as of supreme importance. He may even be fanatical on the subject.

One's reactions to every one of the above statements is colored by his biological make-up, which includes the make-up of his mind. His total reaction to the various statements would indicate whether in the current political situation he is regarded as a "liberal" or a "conservative." Actually, people are often complex mixtures of the two, and it all goes back to a substantial degree to the patterns of their minds. Self-interest and cultural background constitute only a part of the story.

At a recent symposium in Washington under the auspices of the National Academy of Sciences, Dr. Robert Livingston, neurologist of the National Institutes of Health, who presided, made some informal opening remarks which he has allowed me to quote as follows:

> Each of us develops distinctive skills and habits depending on innate equipment and individual experience. These shape new percepts to conform to previous experience by mechanisms that operate on the sense receptors and oncoming sensory signals. Sense data on which our perceptions are based are thus altered long before they reach consciousness. A full and general understanding of this fact could reduce much of the "sonabitchery" we perceive in others.

Ability to communicate with each other is by no means a cure for all human misunderstanding and strife, but it is an essential link. I have been told by experts in the field of communication that the recognition of individuality is of the utmost importance in this area. It is a frustrating error to think of communication as taking place between two hypothetical "average" persons.

George Santayana, the philosopher, recognized intuitively many years ago the innate distinctiveness and spottedness of people's minds when he wrote: "Friendship is almost always the union of a part of one mind with another; people are friends in spots." People agree in spots, people can communicate in spots; in other spots they fail to understand each other or agree. This is an inevitable consequence of the individuality of our thinking. To resort to name-calling— thinking of the supposed sonabitchery of others—is a cheap and shoddy substitute for an intelligent understanding of the basis of the interaction of human minds.

It is true, as someone has said, that people get many of their opinions on public questions by contagion, just as they get colds and other diseases. But what makes this statement subject to qualification is the fact that just as people differ in their susceptibility to colds and other contagious diseases because of individuality in their bodies, they also differ in their susceptibility to ideas because of the individuality of their minds.

My total experience working with my own and others' minds is very much in accord with these concepts. There are some aspects of chemistry, biology and mathematics that I grasp with crystal clarity. There are others that always remain muddy. There are some commonly used words in biology that I cannot incorporate into my vocabulary because they seem to carry with them dubious assumptions that are not even clear to me. This same spottedness exists in students' minds, though they rarely can afford to admit it. Their patterns of mind make it relatively easy for them to accept, digest and assimilate certain ideas. From the time of assimilation on, these ideas influence and color all their thinking. On the other hand, other ideas are sometimes merely memorized; they fall on stony ground, fail to take root, and never become effective in changing a later concept, attitude or opinion.

The world of human communication, including agreement and disagreement, looks entirely different when we consider the facts of inborn individuality. We need to recognize that these facts apply to every situation—whether it is Pope Paul meeting a patriarch of the Greek Church, two neighbors talking across the backyard fence or a husband helping his wife balance her checkbook.

Education takes on what amounts to almost a new dimension when we consider the facts of inborn individuality. For practical reasons and because we want to teach brotherhood and good will, we have striven to treat all children alike. This carries the implication that they *are* all alike. This in turn leaves out of their schooling one of the most useful things that they can know—their own inborn characteristics and aptitudes.

The new dimension in education can best be made clear by pointing out the absurdity of the statement we sometimes hear: "He is a very well educated man but he has made a mess of his life." In the light of the facts of individuality such a person could not exist. If, in this new light, a person is *well* educated, this means that he knows *himself* adequately. If he makes a mess of his life, this is prima-facie evidence that he wasn't well educated. An academic education is different from a real education. An academic education leaves out—largely—the ingredient of knowing one's self. Informally we always learn something about ourselves—but not enough—and usually it is not a planned part of our education.

An educated man may be described, in the light of the facts of individuality, as one who gets the right kind of job, chooses a suitable mate and rears children who grow to be productive, learns to live with himself and to appreciate much that culture offers, knows and appreciates people and knows how to care for his own health. If one gets into the wrong job, marries unwisely, has no peace of mind, gets little out of music, drama, art or literature, likes dogs better than people and ruins his own health, he is poorly educated regardless of how high his academic credits may be stacked.

Children ought to begin at an early age to understand the individuality that they and all others possess. Children of kindergarten age have different ears for pitch, rhythm and melody; each has his own color vision, and in any classroom there will be many different reactions to colors and color combinations; their taste buds will not agree; their judgments regarding a host of odors and flavors will not agree; their reaction times and motor skills—including the way they can use their hands—will be distinctive. Some knowledge about all this could be gained informally and would be a wholesome and early inoculation against the disease that makes people hate anyone who is "different."

As students progress through school—if they are to be really educated, not merely academically educated—they should learn more and more about themselves, and inevitably, as a consequence, more and more about others. They also need to learn something about the many thousands of kinds of jobs that need to be done in our complex modern world. When it is time for them to leave school, at whatever level, they should have enough insight into themselves and the world around them so they will know "where to go from here." If they have not arrived at this stage, they may have an academic education but not the kind of education they need.

This objective is good for everyone whether his or her schooling is limited to grade school or high school or progresses on as far as the postdoctorate level. Everyone needs training, but since people have enormous inborn differences their needs are not met unless many types and grades of education are offered. If in a specific instance the schooling we offer to a youngster appears quite unsuitable—he loathes it —we are likely to do what the doctor did for me when I reacted unfavorably to morphine: prescribe "more of the same" on the assumption that the prescription is bound to be right, and the recalcitrant student must be adjusted, made uniform and brought into line. We have paid dearly in millions of ruined lives by neglecting individuality and those who exhibit it in some inconvenient way.

The complete burden of education in the broadest sense should not be placed upon our academic system. Our homes, churches and synagogues, and outside activities are and always will be of first-order importance. We need, however, in our academic setup more recognition of individuality, and with it will come, naturally, a more wholesome attitude.

Different occupations and different people require differing amounts of academic education. Those who need and receive a large quota of academic training should not feel "uppity" about it. This is offensive. Those whose education includes not so much academic schooling should not feel "downity." This is degrading. Will Rogers said, "We're all ignorant—about different things."

A full recognition of individuality in the education process—it is already recognized to a degree—need not involve any revolution in the mechanics of our schools. Schoolrooms, teachers and pupils associated together may remain unchanged; if the teachers and the public are informed about the facts of inborn individuality, this knowledge will inevitably percolate to the students, and this will help them become truly educated, not merely academically educated.

Delinquency and crime take on quite a different look when we think of them in the light of the facts of individuality.

Sheldon and Eleanor Glueck of Harvard University are noted students of crime and delinquency. They have recently made over four hundred comparisons between delinquent children and comparable children who are not delinquent in order to try to find out why they are the way they are. Their findings include three facts that are of great significance. First, the seeds of delinquency, whatever they are, have already been planted by the time the children are ready for school. Second, the body builds of the children have something to do with delinquency. When the delinquent and control groups were compared it was found that mesomorphs (medium build) were twice as numerous in the delinquent group as in the control group. Ectomorphs (light weight) on the other hand, were only about a third as abundant in the delinquents as in the nondelinquents. Eleanor Glueck said in an interview: "This difference hit us between the eyes." Well it might, because there has been so little attention paid to the possible effects of biological characteristics on human behavior. Third, they found that poverty or living in a slum area was not enough to account for delinquency, because many of the nondelinquents were reared in the same unfavorable environment.

In the light of the facts of individuality, delinquency may be interpreted as follows: Each child is innately endowed with a unique pattern of characteristics. If the child is vigorous and healthy and if he finds in his conventional environment inadequate or inappropriate outlets for his energy, he is likely to become delinquent. Poverty is restrictive and may promote delinquency; the lack of family life, the lack of an understanding father, the lack of a diligent mother compound the difficulty of satisfying innate urges in a restricted, urban environment.

Inborn individuality is a tremendously important factor in the problem. If all children had the same likes and dislikes, it would be relatively easy to satisfy them. An understanding father, for example, would not be so hard to come by because children would be easy to understand. A child who has few strong, compelling and distinctive likes and dislikes will be more easily understood (and may be easier to love) than one who is continually wanting to kick over the traces. Love is a two-way operation. Children who are loving by nature find more love in their homes than do children who, for numerous possible reasons, foster ill feeling toward others.

Among the general population of youngsters there are those, for example, who do not like most traditional school activities. (There are grownups who feel the same way about it; when they finish their schooling, the farther away they can get from an "academic" atmosphere the better.) Of course, one of the things disliked about school is the *work,* but the difficulty in the case of delinquents is not simply laziness. Youngsters who hate one kind of work may be very diligent if the work is of a different kind. I know of a young girl who appeared to be extremely lazy around the house, but when she was given an opportunity to operate a typewriter, she worked at it willingly and did an excellent job. I remember many years ago as a foreman I hired a young man to do manual work for me and with me. He was, and I knew him well, one of the most industrious students of my acquaintance. In working with me manually he turned out to be the laziest person I ever hope to witness, and at sundown I had to relieve him of his duties.

It is difficult to explain fully, but people are like that. I dare say that young adolescents could be found who would exhibit behavior *exactly* the opposite to my physically lazy friend. In school they might be the laziest imaginable, but put them at a job involving the right kind of manual operations and they might appear very industrious. The most effective and almost universal way of making a criminal into a useful citizen is to get him a job *doing something he likes to do.*

Dr. James Devon, a physician in a Scotch prison, wrote over fifty years ago: "There is only one principle in penology that is worth any consideration: it is to find out why a man does wrong and make it not worth his while." This to me rings absolutely true. It becomes evident that the crucial unknown in the problem of delinquency and crime is the individual leanings and desires of those who may become delinquent and criminal. These characteristics can never be found out by studying the hypothetical "normal" child, no matter how exhaustive such a study is.

Delinquent children are not inherently bad. As a group they are probably more distinctive than nondelinquents. They are probably fully as energetic and full of vitality. Their leanings do not usually incline them toward academic work but they are capable nonetheless of being highly productive citizens. Inventiveness—the ability to do things in a new unconventional way—is one of the things we are liable to lose when a child is lost to the criminal class.

Even business is markedly affected in many ways by inborn individuality. To illustrate. It was supposed centuries ago that people could be put simply into two groups: those who were blind and those who could see. Later it developed that another group should be added: those who needed spectacles to correct for the effects of old age. The spectacle business was created at that time. Now we recognize many types of eyes and eye difficulties—and *as a result of the recognition of the tremendous individuality* in people's eyes, a mammoth industry, involving millions of people, has developed. This business will expand much further when we know more about the inherent individuality in people's eyesight.

Many other large businesses have developed because of inborn individuality. The publication of newspapers, magazines and books would amount to little, indeed, were it not for the fact that millions of individuals exist with numerous tastes. No paper, magazine or book has to please everyone to be a success. A book which appeals strongly to one per cent of the population can become a tremendous best seller. Newspapers are not published for the "average reader"; they are published for a great variety of readers, most of whom read only selected parts. The largest newspapers, especially, cater to a tremendous variety of people, including those who pride themselves on being highly intellectual.

The food industry is another that thrives because of inborn individuality. If everybody had the same tastes, there would be no such thing as a supermarket. A breakfast food doesn't need to appeal to everybody in order to be a success. If it is demanded by one out of ten (the other nine might *dislike* it), its sales might be a multimillion dollar business.

There is no such thing as the best beer, the best cigarette, the best mattress, the best soap, the best hairdressing, the best razor, the best laxative, the best house, the best musical composition, the best automobile or the best school. These do not exist any more than does the best novel or the best poem. A great variety of tastes exists with respect to all these and many other products. Thousands of products for which I personally would have no use whatever sell regularly and in large volume.

There would be no future hope for an expanding economy if it were not for inborn individuality and the fact that people are individuals in thousands of ways, and that as they become more affluent they can, to an ever-increasing degree, be catered to accordingly.

The facts of inborn individuality have a great deal to do with government and politics; in fact, our form of government would not exist if the founding fathers had not known intuitively about the basic need of every individual to live his own life.

When the Declaration of Independence states "all men are created equal," it *seems* to deny the existence of inborn individuality, but it does not, as becomes increasingly clear when we read the entire sentence in which this clause appears. What the writers had in mind was expressed more simply in the Virginia Bill of Rights written three weeks before. In this document it was said this way: "All men are by nature equally free and independent." What the colonists objected to strenuously was the *inborn* right claimed by kings, specifically George III, to rule over them. They certainly did not entertain the preposterous idea that every newborn baby is the exact duplicate of every other, but they did hold the opinion, quite correctly, that "royal blood" is an illusion and that no person by birth has the right to rule over another.

They knew intuitively that people are not all alike; otherwise why would they have insisted from early times on the right of each person to have his own religion and to live his own life? Why could Patrick Henry move his audience with the famous "Give me liberty or give me death" speech unless they had the desire for liberty themselves—recognizing that each had vital desires that were not in accord with those of everyone else, and hence could not be satisfied in a regimented environment. The unifying element among the colonists was the desire to grasp the unalienable right of each to life, liberty and the pursuit of happiness—each in his own way. Each was different and the colonists wanted the right to remain so.

If people were all built the same—hearts, muscles, stomachs, endocrine glands, nervous systems, brains—all would have the same abilities, likes and dislikes; people would readily be molded alike; they would not insist on the right to choose their own church, their own books, their own schools, their own amusements. The right to the pursuit of happiness would be the right to remain in a common rut.

If people were different from each other *only in trifling ways*—fingerprints, length of noses, the texture of their hair, the exact shape of their eye lenses—they might insist on wearing their own spectacles and on a few other minor rights. But the rights that Patrick Henry and others were ready to die for were of a very different kind and would never have been thought of if the individuals concerned had not possessed the enormously significant biological individuality which we now know about. This inborn individuality was and is the mainspring of our love of liberty.

The basic idea that human beings are born about alike and are different only because their environments have molded them differently is widely held but is completely untenable in the light of the facts we have presented. The Russian Marxist Nikolai Bukharin has said: "If we examine separate individuals in the process of development, we observe that essentially they are packed with influences of their environment to the same extent that a sausage is filled with meat."

If we accept this point of view, people are like sausages in more than one respect: they can be molded and packed by the state to fill the needs of the state. Individual freedom and the love of liberty go out the window. These fundamental urges cannot go completely out the window even in a Communist state, but the basic idea of individual freedom still is intolerable in the Communist world. When individual freedom becomes important, communism disappears. Even Karl Marx, however, who died long before the Russian revolution, appeared to have some appreciation of the importance of individuality when he wrote: "Russia has only one opponent: the explosive power of democratic ideas, that inborn urge of the human race in the direction of freedom." He continued to think, however, of a crucial mass movement —Labor united against Capital—in which individuality would be completely submerged.

Nothing in human affairs will work out satisfactorily without crucial inborn individuality. Without recognizing it, we cannot communicate or understand our frequent disagreements; we cannot become really educated; we cannot cope with and prevent delinquency and crime. Our expanding economy depends upon it, and the love of liberty which is the keystone of civilization in the Western world cannot exist without it. Communism cannot endure *with* it; the acceptance of potent inborn individuality will shake communism to its foundations.

These observations about the new world which we see in the light of inborn individuality are general and far-reaching. There are also some day-to-day practical problems to which we cannot find solutions until we recognize inborn individuality. These will be discussed in the next two chapters.

CHAPTER VIII

Eating, Drinking, Taking Medication

People should be treated as individuals because they are individuals, and in the common activities of eating and drinking one needs to think of himself as an individual, otherwise serious difficulties are liable to arise.

Part of one's individuality resides in his "body wisdoms," which Walter Cannon, a Harvard physiologist, first wrote about thirty years ago. He described some of the various built-in control mechanisms which regulate our body temperature, our breathing operation, our heart beat, the composition of our blood, our fluid intake, our food intake, etc. The various coordinated "wisdoms" make continued life possible.

Not being aware of the facts of individuality as we have presented them, Cannon wrote in general terms and of course

did not point out that since each of us is built in a highly distinctive manner, the body-wisdom mechanisms of each of us
is also distinctive in its operation. These many mechanisms
do not work with equal efficiency in all of us; they can get
out of order, in which case mild body foolishness—or even
fatal foolishness—can take the place of the "wisdom" we
should have. Like the man-made thermostats, pressure regu-
lators, timers and other control mechanisms we use in our
factories, our body-wisdom mechanisms require *care* and
maintenance.

Fortunately, some of these mechanisms are built so that
barring abuse, they help maintain themselves. When we
exercise freely we perspire and our tissues lose part of the
water they need. This dehydration spreads to the control
center, which produces a sense of thirst; we are impelled to
drink water and the dehydration disappears. All the tissues
including those in the control center are happy again.

However, if we abuse the water-control mechanism too
severely, it may falter and fail, like a jammed thermostat. If
one becomes lost on the desert with a canteen of water, and
determines not to drink any of it until he can stand the thirst
no longer, his dried-out body is likely to be found perhaps
weeks later (as has happened) with a canteen of water nearby.
If the control mechanism becomes too dehydrated, it no
longer produces the sensation of thirst and one may go on
and on with a false sense of security. "Body foolishness" has
really taken over and death results.

Most of us are all too familiar with the fact that we
have a periodic feeling of hunger, which is a manifestation of
the "body wisdom," which keeps us from starving to death.
We may also be aware that this body wisdom turns out to
be a bit on the foolish side when as so often happens with
sedentary people, appetite directs them to eat too much.

What is wrong with the maintenance and why does the

mechanism fail? In this case also the mechanism helps maintain itself, but if it begins to falter, its self-service maintenance may also fail and along with it the maintenance of many other regulating devices.

If one goes on a hunger strike, the sensation of hunger may be acute for a day or two or more; then it may subside and disappear. Too much abuse in the form of impaired nutrition may cause the mechanism to stop operating. It is not necessary that the mechanism be deprived of all food in order that it stop operating. It is well established that withholding a single essential vitamin (vitamin B_1) from fowls, rats or human beings will cripple the working of their appetite mechanisms. If one attempts to keep pigeons on a polished-rice diet, which largely lacks this vitamin, the birds shortly refuse to eat at all and if left alone will die of starvation. The protective antistarvation mechanism fails because of its own malnutrition. It will recover promptly and the pigeons will eat again if they are furnished, by injection or otherwise, the missing vitamin. The tissues involved in the appetite mechanism, sometimes called the "appestat," are peculiarly sensitive to this form of malnutrition; other bodily mechanisms can continue to operate for a considerable period when the animal is on a polished-rice diet. If an outsider takes over the appetite function and regularly stuffs polished rice down the pigeon's throat, the pigeon will live for weeks.

One of the most important things that we human beings can do for ourselves is to keep all our tissues well nourished so that our "body wisdoms" all continue in good working order. Most important of all is the proper nutrition of our babies, children and young adults so that their body wisdoms will all be healthy and they will not be afflicted with self-perpetuating disorders.

I am a fortunate person in that my general appestat mechanism which controls how much food I eat works very satisfactorily. Inasmuch as I like to walk, play golf and billiards and am not able, because of my eyesight, to sit by the hour to read, I am fairly active physically. As a result, when I eat just as much as I feel like, I eat something approaching a ton of moist food in a year. If my appestat were to cause me to eat and assimilate consistently one per cent more than than it does, I would gain at the rate of about twenty pounds per year or two hundred pounds each ten years. My appestat makes no such error as this! Even an error one tenth this great would make me gain twenty pounds in ten years. My weight fluctuates a few pounds, but over the years it doesn't change appreciably. My appestat works so well that it seldom occurs to me to weigh myself. Of course, I try to help the good work along by eating with some wisdom, and when I find that too much supper makes me restless at night, I try eating less with great satisfaction. For some reason which I do not fully understand I am particularly sensitive to too much beefsteak, and anything more than a small portion will make me roll around restlessly at night. This restlessness is a part of my body wisdom which warns me not to repeat the error.

One should take advantage of every clue and every warning that his body wisdoms provide. Many people are often restless and uneasy inside, yet have never discovered that by using the simple expedient of eating far less, their trouble disappears. Keeping up with the Joneses in eating is a foolish practice. If, however, you love eating well enough so that you are willing to accept the discomforts and dangers that excesses bring, then in a free country you should be allowed this pursuit of happiness.

Back in Oregon, when our two older children were small, I distinctly remember we parents had a good-natured argument over whether it would be all right when they were naughty to give each a glass of milk and send them to bed without any further supper. Their mother argued against this; she was afraid they would suffer from hunger and would not sleep well. We tried the experiment; as a result both children slept *unusually well;* in fact, we heard absolutely nothing out of them until late morning, whereas when they had eaten as usual we often were disturbed by them. It would be a good idea if children were made more food-conscious and were made to think about the desirability of eating the right amounts of the right things. It would not hurt if even small children were made to "earn" their evening meal by completing some small daily task before they were allowed to eat. This would make them appreciate food more and be more concerned about getting "their money's worth" in good nutrition.

The lack of a substantial weight-control problem in my case is not mentioned by way of bragging. Actually, many people are in the same boat, and animals in the wild active state also have finely adjusted automatic controls. You don't see squirrels too fat to climb a tree, crows too fat to fly or salmon too fat to swim upstream at spawning time. Even in time of abundant food wild animals know when to stop eating without having any calorie charts to consult. I am told that among domesticated animals mules have far more body wisdom in this regard than horses. Give a hungry starved mule plenty of food and it will know when to stop, but a horse under similar circumstances may kill itself. Thus I must confess to being more like a mule than a horse. The fact remains that in the entire biological kingdom with its many kinds of creatures, appestats or their equivalent *are the rule, not the exception,* and they are often most precise in their regulation of food intake.

People are often prone to take one of two extreme positions with regard to appestat mechanisms—either they are to be trusted as infallible guides, or else they should be completely disregarded. When appestats are regarded as infallible, children are allowed to fill up on sweets and starches as they wish. If appestats are thought of as worthless, parents think they have to stuff a certain amount of food down their children regardless—especially babies. Appestats need to be used when they appear to be sound, and they need to be tempered when they obviously cause too much food consumption or when they call for large amounts of starches and sugars, refined or semirefined foods. These operate to exclude other nutrients that are essential for health. One way in which people show individuality is in their appestats; they are not all the same.

No one knows for sure just why appestats go awry and cause people to eat too much. I have a strong suspicion that an important factor in making appestats get out of adjustment is malnutrition during childhood, and that malnutrition during adulthood continues to aggravate the situation. When I once saw a young boy at a cafeteria choosing, with his mother's approval, a bill of fare consisting of macaroni with a little cheese coloring, a roll, cake and a soft drink for his evening meal, I could see coming up the makings of a disordered appestat as well as the possible derangement of a number of other body functions and wisdoms.

The idea that fully adequate nutrition in early youth paves the way for a happy adult life might be termed "nutritional Freudianism." If an appestat is well nourished from the start (and this should begin prenatally), it seems reasonable that it will remain well adjusted and will help the developing organism to maintain good nutrition.

Excellent nutrition is all-inclusive in its beneficial effects and is essential not only for the regulatory mechanisms but for the development of every organ and tissue—a fact we are inclined to overlook. A common brand of environmentalism leads one to think, for example, that the health of one's teeth depends largely on the manner of brushing and the brand of toothpaste used. We tend to neglect the fact that teeth are most certainly dependent on the *internal* environment—their nutrition—for their development and maintenance. In the laboratory we can produce rats with healthy teeth whenever we wish merely by giving them fully adequate diets. On the other hand, we can produce rats with decaying teeth whenever we wish simply by giving them inadequate diets. The use of toothpastes and regular brushings are usually left out in rat experiments.

Human experience down through the ages jibes with the idea that babies need to be fed with care. Even in the most ignorant circles babies are not expected to subsist on doughnuts and coffee. Building and maintaining the various structures which make possible the numerous body wisdoms is a conspicuous reason for the importance of good early nutrition. This does not mean that later nutrition is *un*important. It remains important as long as we live.

Obesity may well be a disease of malnutrition in which the appestat itself is affected, and because this device is out of adjustment, it prompts us to eat too much food. Never has this problem been attacked in an expert way by investigators fully acquainted with individuality and with the intricacies of nutritional biochemistry.

We possess not only regulating devices which help us decide how much food to eat but also mechanisms which guard us against obviously unwise choices. If we are tempted, for example, to eat great quantities of sugar, our body wisdom throws up a defense and we become nauseated. The same nausea may develop if we are tempted to eat large quantities of fat. We have a well-developed mechanism (involving the adrenal glands) which governs our salt consumption, and if the mechanism is operating correctly it tells us through our taste when we need more salt or less. Your mechanism and mine do not necessarily agree on the amount needed (because our internal construction is not the same); this is why salt shakers are put on dining tables. There is a complex mechanism (involving the parathyroid glands) which governs our appetite for calcium (lime) and also our desire for phosphate.

I remember early in my experience in dealing with experimental animals that I had occasion to deprive rats of the B vitamins for which yeast is a conspicuously good source. I remember offering such a deficient rat, after the experiment was over, a bite of yeast. The little beast was so ravenous that he almost took the end of my finger, too! We probably have a considerable number of internal physiological devices which will help us decide what to eat. These have not been studied adequately partly because they are so *un*uniform among the membership of the human family. Just as our mental faculties are spotted and variable, so also are our numerous body wisdoms. These all need to be kept in working order.

I have a minor defect in my appetite-regulating equipment in that I have a "sweet" tooth—a tendency to consume more sugar than would be best for me. In this respect I have a lot of company, as may be inferred from the amount of candy that is sold, the number of other sweet things that are offered for sale and the number of foods that are "seasoned" with sugar. This part of one's regulatory apparatus has an anatomical and physiological basis. In diabetics, for example, this part of the appetite mechanism often becomes deranged, and there results a strong and perverted appetite for sugar even though a diabetic has great difficulty metabolizing or burning up anything of a carbohydrate nature. Furthermore, this regulating mechanism can be jarred out of adjustment if it suffers from malnutrition. Children who are poorly nourished eat more candy when it is offered to them than those who are well nourished. In our laboratory we have shown that this works the same way with experimental rats; the amount of candy (sugar) they voluntarily consume increases when their diet is made deficient.

One may ask, "What is wrong with eating extra sugar [or starch] if you enjoy it?" The answer is that sugar furnishes "naked" calories (unaccompanied by minerals, amino acids and vitamins) and tends to crowd out of the diet, in both children and adults, good wholesome foods which contain these vital nutrients that are essential for health and for the maintenance of all our body-wisdom devices. One tends to eat just enough calories per day to fill his fuel needs; if these calories are taken in the form of sugar (or starch or alcohol), other food calories are left out, and malnutrition results. This, in individual cases, may be either mild or severe.

Rats as they are raised in laboratories are *un*uniform anatomically just as human beings are. As a result of this, their whole appestat systems are different one from the other and they eat very differently when confronted with different food choices. In a recent experiment in our laboratories a group of rats, caged individually, were given a cafeteria selection of seven foods. Some rats ate consistently four times as much meat as others; some ate consistently seven times as much butter as others; some seventeen times as much sugar and some forty-six times as much fortified yeast. Each rat had an eating pattern of its own. Someone recently tried this out with a group of students and found that each ate distinctively when offered a cafeteria selection.

These differences in the rats must be due, at least in part, to their possession of distinctive hormonal patterns, because we find that their individual eating patterns can be changed by administering various hormones. This is in line with the fact that various appetite mechanisms (such as the appetite for salt and calcium) are known to be tied in with endocrine activities.

Because of the *un*uniformity of their respective metabolic mechanisms, laboratory rats differ markedly in their nutritional needs. We carried out an experiment recently in which groups of rats were given an exclusive diet of enriched white bread to see how they would fare individually on it. One of the simplest ways of judging the well-being of young rats is to note how fast they grow and gain weight. At one end of the scale one weanling rat, weighing initially about forty grams, was able to gain only two grams on this diet and then died. In contrast, one rugged individual starting at the same weight gained over a hundred times as much—212 grams. The gains of the other rats (about sixty of them) were all distributed rather evenly between these two extremes. It is clear, indeed, that this particular diet was far more deficient for some rats than for others, and therefore that rats have highly distinctive individual needs.

This experiment gives us a strong hint that babies and children vary greatly in their susceptibility to the bad effects of a poor diet. If so, we might be relatively careless in the feeding of *some* children without causing catastrophic damage if we knew in advance which ones could take it. But we don't know in advance; the prudent thing is to feed every child so that he or she will get plenty of the crucial things: minerals, proteins (amino acids), vitamins and certain essential fat acids. Consumption of starches and sugars needs to be held down. Not to do so is comparable to trying to run a car with plenty of gasoline and little oil. Since children differ in the amount and quality of the "oil" they need, the only safe practice is to supply each child with plenty of nonfuel nutrients as insurance against malnutrition.

Observation of animals on deficient diets makes me realize that *all sorts* of difficulties may arise from poor nutrition.

Among animals of many species an inevitable accompaniment of poor nutrition is a disheveled appearance and lack of grooming. When their diets are excellent, animals and fowls are sleek and seem to care, psychologically, how they look. When I see unwashed, disheveled beatniks with ragged pants and shirttails, I wonder whether lack of proper diet is not a basic cause of their sad state.

The problem of public education with respect to nutrition is one in which I have a great deal of interest. A little paperback book of mine, *Nutrition in a Nutshell,* has been given by one foundation to nearly 50,000 medical and dental students all over the world with the hope that it will make them more nutrition-conscious. In order to make the book widely acceptable, I did not stress in it the problem of individuality in nutrition. This is a subject for which most scientists are not yet prepared. While this book on nutrition has attained substantial distribution—labor unions have purchased 20,000 copies for distribution to members—and has received hearty endorsement by a large number of the most knowledgeable experts in the world, its contents remain unknown to the vast majority of people including, unfortunately, most physicians.

The fact that there are so many poorly informed nutrition enthusiasts and food faddists tends to work against the acceptance of common-sense ideas about nutrition. Reputable physicians often avoid overt interest in nutrition for fear that they may be considered in the same class as those medical quacks who come up every so often with a catchy best seller on nutrition which is scientifically questionable if not disreputable.

The President's Council on Physical Fitness has justifiably emphasized the importance of physical exercise as a conditioner for youth. They have had virtually nothing to say about good nutrition, which is also a vital need. I suggest that others do as I have done, namely, write urging that this phase of the well-being of youth also be given due attention. I have also corresponded with the director of the National Institutes of Health, urging that more attention be given to nutrition in this vast governmental agency. Sooner or later nutrition will surely receive more attention than it does at present.

The Food and Drug Administration has in the past exhibited in its pronouncements and proposed rulings an unfortunate attitude, to which I have made a formal protest. As late as 1966 it was proposed that it be made compulsory for all vitamin and food supplements to be labeled prominently thus: "Vitamins and minerals are supplied in abundant amounts by the foods we eat . . ."

This labeling, which we understand is likely to be abandoned, carries the implication that no problem exists with respect to nutrition, and that one doesn't even have to eat wisely to get an "abundance" of everything one needs. One can sympathize with the interest of the Food and Drug Administration in protecting the public against exploiters of public ignorance, but to take a blanket position barring the legitimate use of nutritional supplements is like throwing out the baby with the bath.

In my protest to the Food and Drug Administration, I have urged that they cannot deny the validity of the principle of *insurance*. We do not buy fire insurance because we *know* we are going to have a fire. We do not fasten our seat belts because we *know* that the car or plane in which we ride is going to be involved in an accident. A batter in a baseball game does not wear a hard protective cap because he *knows* that he is going to be hit on the head with a pitched ball. There surely must be left room in our country for the legitimate sale of nutritional insurance in the form of food supplements. The use of such supplements need not rest on *knowing* that we are deficient. The facts of individuality suggest strongly that deficiencies are widespread and that nutritional insurance makes sense.

I feel that many food industries have been remiss in that they often do not have real experts on their staff and hence are not in a position to *lead the way* toward better nutrition. Some advertisements for breakfast foods carry the implication that food requirements are based on alleged government pronouncements and not at all on sound biology. The whole public, including those in the food industries, in government agencies and in the medical profession, needs a more liberal and realistic education on the subject of nutrition.

Next let us think about alcohol consumption. This has engaged the attention of some of the workers in my laboratory for about twenty years.

If one puts rats on a stock diet and gives them a choice between water and dilute alcohol as their beverage, they will show enormous differences in their appetites for alcohol. Some will be strict teetotalers even though they have to sniff and choose to avoid it; at the other end of the scale others will become heavy drinkers.

Furthermore, it has been found that rats have as a part of their complete appestat system a regulatory mechanism which governs alcohol consumption and that this device can be turned up or down like a thermostat by altering the nutrition of the animals. It could probably be turned up and down by administering the right hormones to the right animals, but changing the nutrition is a more general procedure, is easier and highly effective. Poor nutrition fosters alcohol consumption (just as it does sugar consumption) and good nutrition diminishes or abolishes it. The stock diet is evidently quite satisfactory for some animals but is relatively deficient for others. The turning up and down of animals' appetite for alcohol by changed nutrition has been done hundreds of times in our and other laboratories; there is no question about it.

While on a stock diet some rats are teetotalers; we have tried to "drive them to drink" by putting jangling cowbells and flashing lights going night and day near their cages. The result: some of the rats are disturbed enough so that even on the stock diet, which is ordinarily adequate for them, they drink alcohol; others, however, maintain their "virtue."

In another laboratory certain cats have been frustrated to such an extent that they voluntarily turned to alcohol consumption. In our experience with experimental animals, poor nutrition is a most effective way of inducing alcohol consumption; frustration may often work, however, in the same direction as deficient nutrition. When experimental animals are frustrated or annoyed, or even isolated and left entirely alone, it modifies their body chemistry in ways that can be measured and changes their nutritional situation. Their need for certain nutrients has been found to increase when they are under stress. So regardless of how it is accomplished, the drinking of alcohol by experimental animals probably involves the malnutrition and consequent malfunctioning of the appetite-regulating system. The *appetite* for alcohol is in any event promoted.

In human alcoholics the entire appetite-regulating device may become defective—not just that portion which governs alcohol consumption—as is evidenced by the fact that alcoholics often show a strong aversion for food of any kind.

When we carried out animal experiments we were not concerned with "alcoholism" in rats. This is no problem. Rats do not get drunk, abuse their families and lose their jobs. We thought that rat experiments would throw light on the essential problem of human alcoholism—the craving for alcohol and the inability to leave it alone. This hope has been justified.

When we found that abundantly good nutrition would prevent alcohol consumption in rats, we immediately asked ourselves: Can abundantly good nutrition abolish the alcohol craving that alcoholics experience? We sought to find the answer by trials, and in every trial we have made or know of where abundantly good nutrition has been attained, there has come a positive answer: Yes, abundantly good nutrition can abolish craving for alcohol by human as well as animal subjects!

There are obstacles, however, to getting our recommendations tried. First, most people are uninformed about nutrition, if they are interested in it at all. So much is to be learned in medical schools that there is often nothing but a stepmotherly treatment of nutrition, and the physicians-to-be cannot get a real grasp of nutritional biochemistry.

As a result of this prevailing lack of expert knowledge, abundantly good nutrition is not always recognizable or distinguishable from faddist notions. Very often, for example, people think that one selection of vitamins or minerals is about as good as another (their physicians may even tell them this); consequently, many very widely sold products cannot pass informed scrutiny. Many who have trouble with alcohol think that they have given abundantly good nutrition a trial if they eat carelessly and supplement this sporadically for a week or two with almost anything that comes in a bottle labeled "vitamins." Actually, what is needed is a continuous intake of plenty of good protein: meat, cheese, eggs, milk, etc.; sparing amounts of refined and starchy foods: sugars, syrups, candies, bread, crackers, cake, etc.; and a good supply of green and/or yellow vegetables. Some unsaturated fat (oil) is desirable in salad dressings. On top of this, for safety a well-

balanced nutritional supplement containing the right vitamins and minerals in about the right amounts should be
taken *regularly* for at least several months. Good results may
come much sooner than this, but continued diligence is necessary.

Another nutritional supplement—glutamine (it is not
a drug)—has proved in some cases to be of great benefit in
abolishing the craving for alcohol. Some confirmed alcoholics
have had their appetite for alcohol taken away from them as
a result of getting this substance in their drinking water
with no knowledge that they were getting anything. (It is a
relatively tasteless substance.) Glutamine is an unusual nutrient in that it is the only amino acid (derived from proteins)
which readily passes the "blood brain barrier" and thus gets
easily into the brain. It is highly important in brain metabolism. Adding it to the diet decreases voluntary alcohol consumption by experimental animals.

Of course, the goal of an alcoholic should be to live with
peace of mind without alcohol or the need for it. There may
be alcoholics who are too sick to want to reach this goal. Unless they have friends or relatives to help them, the problem
becomes hopeless. However, many, many alcoholics want
desperately in their sober moments to get out of the trap they
are in. In my opinion there is an excellent chance that following the suggestions given above will bring them release.
It hurts me to know this and to have the victims remain in
ignorance.

It also hurts me to know that a multitude of young and
middle-aged people are *on the way* to becoming alcoholics
and nothing is being done to head them off. It usually takes
several years of heavy drinking to produce an alcoholic. *All
during* this time the rules of good nutrition are being violated. One drink after another spells poor nutrition regardless of who does the drinking. The fact that some people can

get away with poor nutrition doesn't prevent others from being damaged. We are individuals. Those who are content to let people hit bottom as alcoholics first before attempting to help them have a serious responsibility on their shoulders.

Before anything was known about biochemical individuality it was decided that alcoholism was a psychiatric problem, and attitudes on such a question change slowly. As a result of this psychiatric emphasis, information about the nutritional approach often fails to percolate down to the alcoholics who need the help. (Any reader who has trouble with alcohol can write to the writer personally and receive further specific information in a plain envelope, without charge.)

Historically, the problem of alcoholism has not been considered as involving *individuals.* During the time when prohibition rose and fell the "drys" took the position that since some people become drunkards, all are in danger of it, and prohibition is the only answer. The "wets" on the other hand said that since some people are able to enjoy liquor without apparent damage, *all* should be able to do so. Therefore, prohibition is nonsense. What is needed in this problem, as in many others, is a recognition of inborn individuality. Some are vulnerable and others are not.

Alcoholics Anonymous implies a recognition of inborn differences in their prayer: "God grant me the *serenity* to accept the things I cannot change, *courage* to change the things I can, and *wisdom* to know the difference." The one thing they cannot change is their vulnerability to alcohol, because it is part of their inborn make-up.

There are many inborn characteristics which enter into problems related to eating and drinking. While it is true that tastes can often be cultivated, and are subject to psychological influences, the changes that take place are limited by one's own inborn taste mechanisms. It has been proved conclusively that certain synthetic organic chemicals known as *thioureas* are tasteless to some individuals and extremely bitter to others, and that the differences are based upon heredity. Populations all over the world have been studied in this regard; in some regions nearly 100 per cent get a bitter taste from "PTC" (phenylthiocarbamide); in other regions the percentage is as low as fifty per cent. The percentages within different races differ, but each race has tasters and nontasters within its group.

Sodium benzoate, which is sometimes used as a preservative in catsup and other condiments, causes a wide variation in response when tasted by different individuals. To some it tastes bitter; to others it is sweet; others pronounce it salty, sour or tasteless. The responses in this case are sometimes indefinite and have not been subjected to extensive study.

If one studies carefully the ability of people to taste sugar, salt, saccharin, quinine, cascara, hydrochloric acid (present in gastric juice) or anything else, he will find enormous differences in sensitivity. We must conclude in the light of all the known facts, including those concerned with the variable distribution and efficiency of nerve receptors, that inborn factors play a prominent role in all taste reactions.

Sensitivities to odors (flavors) are often also highly individual, but these have not been studied extensively. About twenty per cent of the males tested were unable to smell hydrocyanic acid (a poisonous gas) under prescribed conditions, as compared with about four per cent for females. This involves sex-linked inheritance. The odors of flowers (verbenas) have been found to elicit strikingly variable responses. In a careful experiment one individual was found to rate a series of verbenas one, two, three, four in terms of their fragrance, while another investigator consistently rated them in exactly the reverse order!

Other facts pertinent to individuality in eating and drinking include known variabilities with respect to human needs for calcium and for several essential amino acids. Various vitamin needs vary also but less definite information is available.

Much more knowledge is needed in this field, because as a result of it, the time may come when *considering the differences between people,* we will be able to answer *for individuals* such questions as: Exactly how can I feed my Mary so as to insure her against obesity? Considering my own distinctive metabolism, how can I eat in such a way as to be certain of avoiding obesity? How can my arthritis be helped nutritionally? How can my tendency toward mental depression be corrected—even partially—by taking care of my individual nutrition? How can I use nutrition to correct the tendency toward dental decay in Tommy's case? How can I, by fulfilling my own peculiar nutritional needs, guard against a stroke or a heart attack that may be in store for me? How can I alter my individual nutrition so as to diminish or abolish my allergies?

All these and other health measures may become possible if we recognize nutritional individuality. If we continue to try to solve such problems on the basis of the average man, we will be continuously in a muddle, because the concept of "the average man" is a muddle. Such a man does not exist.

Knowledge of the elementary facts about individuality in eating and drinking will contribute greatly to our understanding, appreciation and tolerance of others. We will know that people's tastes differ, partly for biological reasons, and should not be the basis for dispute or sonabitchery. "The wild vicissitudes of taste" become not so wild and the saying "no accounting for tastes" becomes obsolete.

Recognizing biochemical individuality, we can accept the fact that Winston Churchill violated many of the rules of good nutrition and lived magnificently in old age, without jumping to the conclusion that nutrition is unimportant for other individuals, including ourselves. Recognizing inborn differences in body chemistry will make commonplace the fact that some individuals should fear the use of alcohol while others have almost no chance of becoming addicted to it. We can perhaps ultimately understand *why* Jack Spratt could eat no fat, and appreciate the insight of the Roman Lucretius, who wrote about two thousand years ago: "What is food to one man may be fierce poison to others."

Ideally, medicines should be taken only with the expert advice of physicians. Actually, however, more medicine is taken without such advice than with it. Unless those who practice self-medication take into account inborn individuality, serious trouble may result. Salt, water, sugar, proteins (which yield amino acids), vitamins or necessary minerals are not medicines in the sense that I am using the word; they are *nutrients* which furnish the body energy or natural ingredients which are essential to life. Any chemical other than a nutrient that we take into our bodies, regardless of why we take it, may be regarded as a "medicine."

Medicinal substances, when taken into the body, either interfere with or modify the body chemistry of the person who takes them or alter the biochemical workings of some bacterial or other parasite. Very often valuable (and not so valuable) medicines have been discovered by trial and error, and darkness prevails as to just how they act. Most drugs, in the ultimate, affect the working of enzymes, those universal catalysts which promote most of the chemical events that take place in our bodies. Since the number of these enzymes is very large and they are located in a host of different cells, it is small wonder that in most cases we do not know exactly how the drug does its work. We can be sure, however, that unless the substance interferes with some part of the metabolic machinery, it is powerless to do anything.

That drug-taking is related to nutrition is evident in the recent case of thalidomide poisoning which resulted in widespread birth defects. This drug was supposed to be harmless but is now known to interfere with that part of the metabolic machinery which involves some of the B vitamins. Similar deformities result if these vitamins are not present in sufficient amounts in the diet.

Aspirin is one of the most widely purchased medicines and is a case in which the mode of action is unknown; it has been used as a medicine during most of the twentieth century; thousands of tons are used annually in this country— yet no one knows (or cares too much!) how it works or why it is such a valuable remedy for such a variety of ailments. Some people consider aspirin as an item to be included regularly in their grocery list.

Because drugs must affect enzyme mechanisms, and since by inheritance each of us has a body chemistry that is unique and different, it follows that we are affected in different ways by the same drug. Aspirin is an especially valuable and widely used medication partly because it is *relatively* uniform in its action. As the advertisements on the radio truthfully say: "It is used by millions of normal people without bad effects." Even aspirin, however, is not completely uniform in its action. Often it is harmless even when taken in mild overdoses, yet it is estimated that about two hundred people die each year from its use—one for about each ten tons of aspirin that is consumed nationally.

My experience with aspirin is that it is effective as a preventive of a cold (or at least certain colds) when I take it at the first signs of throat irritation. Taken later during the progress of a cold it brings temporary relief, and when taken at bedtime it makes breathing easier and allows me to sleep. Since I am not usually subject to headaches, I do not take it for relief of this ailment.

A striking fact is that unless I take plenty of water— one and a half glasses per five-grain tablet—it gives me distressing "heartburn" (so named because it has nothing to do with the heart!). I never take more than one tablet at a time, because this is plenty *for me*, and one glass of water with it is not enough to prevent "heartburn." Other people I know find aspirin no good for colds; some take several tablets at a time and use only enough water to permit swallowing, and never get heartburn. Some people cannot take it because their hearts flutter and act up immediately as a result.

The point of this is: if you take aspirin you may need to learn the art of taking it in the right dosage, at the right time, with the right amount of water and for the right ailments, *all for your own individual case.* The routine directions printed on the package may work for you or they may not. The chances are rather slim that the recommended doses will be good *in your case* for everything that aspirin is used for.

Our bodies are inconceivably complex in that there are hundreds of different kinds of cells with different functions, any and all of which may be affected if allowed to come in contact with a foreign drug.

Our bodies start developing from a single fertilized egg cell about the diameter of a pin; before development (differentiation) is complete there are hundreds of kinds of cells of varying shapes and sizes, differing in composition and in function. The total population of the cell "community" which constitutes each human individual is many trillions; this is thousands of times the human population of the earth.

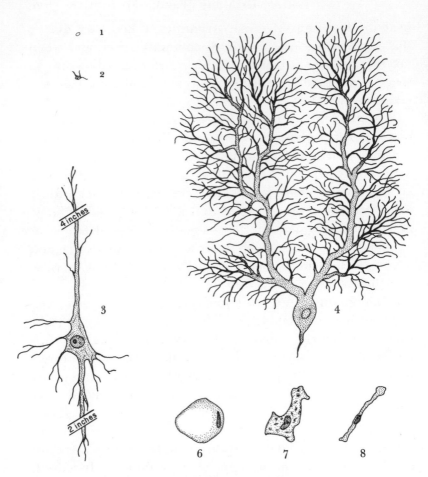

Representative Human Cells x 200

1. Granule cell (brain) 2. Cortical cell (brain) 3. Pyramid cell (brain)
4. Purkinje cell (brain) 5. Motor nerve cell (spinal cord) 6. Fat cell
7. Connective tissue cell 8. Another connective tissue cell 9. Visual
cell, rod (retina) 10. Visual cell, cone (retina) 11. Sensory nerve
cell (ear) 12. Skeletal muscle cell (These are unusual cells in that
each one may have hundreds of nuclei. The asterisk (*) denotes the fact
that such a cell at 200 magnification may be a "pencil" as long as 200
feet.) 13. Muscle cell (heart) 14. Smooth (involuntary) muscle cell
15. Cell (bone marrow) 16. Bone cell 17. Epithelial cell (intestine)
18. Epithelial cell (nose) 19. Red blood cells 20. White blood cells.

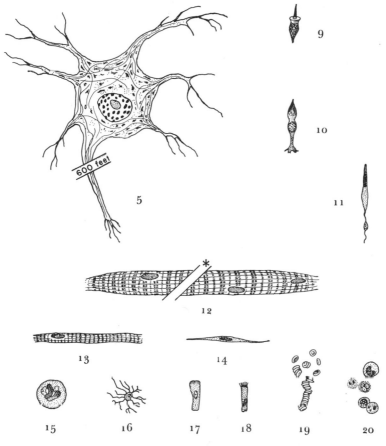

All of the twenty types of human cells represented on the two pages (and many more) are produced by cell division and "differentiation" from a single globular "mother cell" which at this magnification would be about two inches across. Each cell in our body requires day-to-day adequate nutrition and is capable of being poisoned by foreign chemicals.

*A skeletal muscle drawn to this scale may be a "pencil" as long as 200 feet. These are unusual cells in that each one may have hundreds of nuclei. On the other hand, the most numerous cells in our bodies (red blood cells) contain *no* nuclei.

Twenty representative different types of cells—all drawn on the same scale—are shown on pages 130, 131. Of the red blood cells alone (the most numerous), the total number in a human body may be more than thirty trillion.

These cells all require nutrition and all can be poisoned by contact with a drug. To answer the question whether one takes enough of a drug for it to get to all the numerous cells —a five-grain aspirin tablet contains about 1,000,000,000,-000,000,000,000 molecules; this is enough to furnish something like twenty million molecules for each cell in our bodies.

All of these cells are related to each other biochemically and carry on many of their processes in a similar manner, so that a drug which affects one type of cell is likely to affect many others as well. Furthermore, living cells throughout nature are related biochemically to each other, so that what is poison to one kind is likely to be poisonous—to a degree— to others.

For example, if one is infected with parasitic worms in the intestine, they cannot be poisoned by using a hammer-and-tongs approach, because the same poisons that will kill the parasites will also kill the person who carries them. What must be done therefore is to search for poisons which are relatively impotent so far as human beings are concerned and relatively potent for the parasite which one wishes to destroy.

Antibiotics are marvelously effective drugs for the treatment of bacterial infections; they do not kill bacteria, but bacterial growth and multiplication are inhibited and the body is able to dispose of them. Antibiotics interfere with the normal biochemical goings-on in bacterial cells by interfering with enzymes. But similar enzymes are likely to be present in our bodies also, and the normal goings-on in our healthy cells and tissues can be interfered with seriously by antibiotics. Many people are made very ill and even die as the result of the administration of specific antibiotics.

When one goes to a hospital now, one of the first questions asked is whether or not there are any antibiotics that cannot be tolerated. If and when I go to the hospital next time I hope I can remember to tell them not to give me "furadantin," because this antibiotic nearly killed me the last time I was given it and my doctor told me to be sure never to run this risk again.

In recent decades it has become common knowledge that penicillin—also other antibiotics—may cause a mild rash or severe reactions, even death. "Antihistaminics" are also known to yield diverse reactions in different individuals. Benadryl in one study caused side reactions in 133 out of 217 individuals to whom it was given. Drowsiness happened in 94 cases, dry mouth in 44, itching or burning on the hands in 32, headache in 21, dizziness in 15, nervousness in 8, ringing in the ears in 8, vomiting in 4, confusion in 3, 2 were made uncontrollably sleepy, 2 were made weak and 1 suffered from diarrhea. Some, of course, had more than one symptom at the same time.

Benadryl is not exceptionally bad in this regard; every antihistaminic causes side reactions in a somewhat comparable way. The variation in the symptoms in this case shows how the same drug may have effects on various cells and tissues and in different locations and in different individuals because of the uniqueness of different body chemistries. A drug which is capable of being beneficial in one way is also capable of being harmful in other ways.

In recent years the use of tranquilizing drugs has presented the medical profession with many examples of striking diversity of response. No one who works with these agents expects anything like uniformity. This was emphasized by

David Krech, University of California psychologist, who recently summarized in a humorous vein a panel discussion by presenting his "first three laws of psychopharmacology" (this is the science which has to do with the psychological effects of drugs). His first law states that *no generalizations* can be made about the biochemical control of the complex human mind. The second law is that there are many exceptions to the first law. The third law is that the first and second laws hold only for extreme cases, except where they do not hold. This area of psychopharmacology is one in which biochemical individuality really shows its head in a convincing manner.

We are beginning now to come closer to an answer to the specific question which was posed early in this book: Why did I react in a peculiar fashion to morphine?—a question that was the starting point for a series of other questions. Clearly, it was due to something different about the chemistry of my nervous system. In the light of the facts about individuality which we have presented, an idiosyncrasy such as this one should come as no surprise. In a recent study of the effects of a carefully controlled dose of morphine on 29 healthy students, it reportedly caused nausea in 18, sleep in 16, "drunkenness" in 9, dizziness in 13, itching in 9 and indistinct speech in 7. It may be noted that there were 72 symptoms and only 29 students. This means that many of the students exhibited more than one symptom. The racing of the mind in the absence of sleep—my reaction—was not noted in any of these cases; perhaps if 100 or 200 students had been tested, this would have been observed.

From the standpoint of understanding addictions to various drugs, it is essential that we recognize the biochemical individuality of the victims and the nature of their vulnerability. We cannot deal with the problem intelligently as long as we think of it in terms of hypothetical "man" and neglect the crucial fact that individual reactions are very far from uniform.

The problem of crime is intimately associated with that of dope addiction because our way of handling narcotic drugs puts addicts in a position where they have to steal and rob in order to satisfy their craving. If the roots of addiction, which lie in the realm of individuality, can be ferreted out, great progress can be made in preventing addiction and in the proper handling of those who are already addicts. Progress in preventing addictions would mean a tremendous decrease in crime.

It is a fact which no informed person can argue about, that there is no drug or chemical agent known that will give uniform results when tested on a substantial number of people. Chemists who are making new compounds all the time, some of them for possible medicinal use, may dream about coming up with a uniformly beneficial chemical which will have no untoward effects on anyone, but this, in view of what we know about metabolic machinery and biochemical individuality, is an idle dream—as idle as the dream of perpetual motion.

Chemists are continually producing a host of new chemicals that never appeared on this planet before. Many of these have no probable medical uses and have not and will not be tested for their physiological effects. Those chemists who are interested in producing new and useful drugs have them tested on animals first. If the results are very irregular, the compound is discarded. Only those agents which are found to be relatively uniform in their effects are worth exploring further, and few of these survive for actual use. Thousands of discarded drugs would, if used, demonstrate the facts of individuality more dramatically than the drugs we have retained.

One of the devices used to try to insure uniformity in action by a drug item is to put several similar agents into the same pill. How clear-cut the objective is, is not certain, but the effect is that what one ingredient will not do for a particular individual, another similar-acting ingredient may. One cold remedy that I know of contains aspirin and an antihistaminic, both of which may be beneficial for colds in different ways and perhaps in different individuals; it also contains caffeine, presumably to counteract the drowsiness which the antihistaminic may produce. So far as I am concerned, both the aspirin and the antihistaminic are effective and beneficial, but I am sensitive to caffeine—it keeps me awake when I want to sleep—so I do not use this otherwise excellent cold remedy. I purchase aspirin and the antihistaminic and use them separately.

Arguments about whether caffeine keeps one awake are based on an acceptance of the idea of uniformity. Those who accept this idea say, "Either it does or it doesn't." If one happens to be nonsensitive, he says, "I *know* it doesn't keep me awake; I'm sure it can't keep others awake. It must be in their minds." This overlooks the fact that the amounts of a drug necessary to bring about the same effect in different individuals may often vary as much as tenfold. There is also the complication that individuals are not always consistent with themselves. At certain times one may be far more sensitive than at others.

It is, however, true that people are often subject to suggestion. If given a sugar pill and told that it contained caffeine, some individuals would be kept awake. The use of placebos (blank pills) has been studied rather extensively in various connections, and depending on the conditions of the experiment, the reported positive responses have been all the way from four per cent up to fifty-two per cent of the people tested. Susceptibility to suggestion is closely allied to the ease with which people undergo hypnosis. Here people vary greatly; they are by no means uniform.

Nicotine—a drug which people use whenever they use tobacco—is another substance which is highly variable in its results. It causes in rare individuals the development of blind areas in the retina (amblyopia); in other rare cases it causes Buerger's disease—impaired circulation in the lower extremities which often necessitates amputation.

Raymond Pearl, many years ago in a study involving nearly 7,000 men, showed that heavy smoking decreased longevity very markedly if one started statistically with a group thirty years of age. Half of the heavy smokers in such a group were dead by the time they reached age fifty-seven, while half of the nonsmokers were not dead until age sixty-eight. He uncovered strong evidence in opposition to the uniformity idea, because in spite of the tremendous advantage of the nonsmokers, when the statistics started at age thirty, he found that if he compared heavy smokers and nonsmokers considering only those who had reached seventy years of age, there was little difference between the heavy smokers and the nonsmokers. The obvious and reasonable interpretation, on the basis of what we now know about biochemical individuality, is that those whose length of life is decreased by tobacco were practically all dead by the age of seventy; from this point on, the investigator was comparing extra-resistant individuals (whom smoking has not seriously harmed) with other individuals of the same age and similar life expectancy. They came out about a tie.

Recent interest in the relationship between lung cancer and cigarette smoking has brought to light further evidence in opposition to the uniformity idea which is so often tacitly accepted. While there can be no reasonable doubt that cigarette smoking is associated with a common type of lung cancer, it remains a fact that all are not equally susceptible— among men it has been estimated that one heavy smoker in ten gets lung cancer. Among women the incidence is less.

Why are the majority of smokers—nine out of ten—resistant? It must be due to differences in body chemistry—lack of uniformity in the human species. In our laboratories we have taken some first steps to try to find out by what biochemical earmarks we can tell susceptible from nonsusceptible individuals. Unfortunately for the tobacco growers and manufacturers, there are other ways in which tobacco contributes to mortality—notably in connection with heart disease. Because of the way we are built, resistance to lung cancer on the part of an individual would not confer resistance against heart disease. Heavy smoking will decrease longevity probably for several reasons. Each person is susceptible and resistant in his own way. Fortunately for the tobacco interests, people love the weed in spite of its bad effects. When I was in college one of my close friends smoked heavily. He called cigarettes "coffin nails" and perhaps they are—he has long since passed on. The idea that cigarettes are harmful is not a new idea. There does seem to be something of a concerted effort now to curb the desire of youngsters to start smoking. Whether this can be successful in the face of the example of their elders and the advertising that is prevalent is questionable.

Another way in which individuality must enter into this problem has to do with addiction. Some smokers can hardly be classed as addicts, since their withdrawal symptoms, if any, are mild; they do not tend to increase their consumption as time goes on; and if they become convinced through their doctor or otherwise that smoking is bad for them, they quit and that is that.

Others, however, are really addicted and the desire to smoke is so compelling that they are unable to cope with it. The situation is not too much unlike that of morphine addiction or alcohol addiction. One of my former students told me of his agonizing and finally successful attempt to stop cigarettes. After a year or so of not smoking he thought he would try smoking *occasionally*. Now he is going full tilt again and has no hope of ever being able to quit. He hopes, of course, that he is one of those who is resistant to tobacco with respect to lung cancer, heart disease, amblyopia, Buerger's disease or anything else it may promote.

It would be worthwhile finding out what is peculiar about the body chemistry of those who are not susceptible to tobacco addiction, but this is inherently hard to do—especially so in a climate where inborn differences are looked upon as being doubtful or perhaps even immoral. Possibly if we knew what was involved in natural resistance to tobacco addiction, we could confer this resistance upon others.

I have the good fortune to possess the characteristics, whatever they are, that make tobacco addiction impossible or at least highly improbable. I had older brothers who smoked; I looked up at them and thought that smoking was a badge of manhood. I lived in California during my adolescence, where it was illegal to sell tobacco to minors, and I respected this law. The day I became twenty-one, however, I went to a tobacconist in Berkeley, where I was in graduate school, and prepared to become a participant in the manly art of smoking. For reasons which I now regard as being tied in with my biochemical individuality, I smoked only a few times and then quit. For a number of years I made it a practice to smoke one cigarette a year just for sociability and to prove (I suppose) that I was not "peculiar." Even this practice petered out. Smoking never had any attraction for me. Cigarettes (unfiltered then) were like hay in my mouth. Thank God for that.

Drugs and medicines—these are foreign to our body—cannot be taken regularly day after day, month after month and year after year with safety, no matter what they are. If they have any drug action at all, consistent use will demonstrate eventually that they are unsafe. People who take it upon themselves to consume with regularity aspirin or other headache remedies, or antihistaminics, or sleeping pills (of any variety) or tranquilizers or laxatives or reducing pills or any other kind of drug are subjecting themselves to danger. There are no drugs that do not have side effects.

This is one of the reasons I have made a strong plea for recognition of the difference between drugs and nutritional substances. The latter are natural to our bodies and are perfectly safe when used in reasonable amounts. These nutritional substances we should get from our food, but because of our biochemical individuality and the differences in our needs, nutritional supplements which serve as insurance make some sense. These can be taken consistently day after day and year after year with perfect safety, provided the amounts are suitable. No informed person can put limitations, in advance, on what a given essential nutrient can do. It is likely to be needed by any and every cell in the entire body and hence its beneficial effects may be in any and every possible direction.

Drugs and medicines can work in many directions, too. In one of our national magazines there were enumerated and pictured (with at least a hint of satire) eight bona-fide "blessings of our time": (1) a pill to prevent sunburn; (2) a pill to keep mosquitoes away; (3) a pill to ease your pain; (4) a pill to keep you awake; (5) a pill to put you to sleep; (6) a pill which helps you stop smoking; (7) a pill that helps you lose weight; (8) a pill that keeps you from getting pregnant. To these should be added (9) a pill to make you happy (tranquil).

All these pills work, after a fashion, on specific individuals, and the usefulness of the majority of them on occasion is undoubted. None of them can be free from side effects and none is safe as a steady diet. The advance of civilization does not center on finding better and better pills. A pill-bound advance toward Utopia sounds like an impractical and not very alluring dream.

Because of the potential dangers, the administration of drugs and medicines should be in the hands of physicians. Especially as people become versed in the elements of hygiene, they may be trusted to treat themselves for minor ailments—people should not run to a physician every time they sniffle—but the continued use of any drug (and the use of many of them under any circumstances) should be under expert medical supervision. Doctors generally discourage their patients from taking any drug continuously for an indefinite period.

One of the general observations one can make in the light of the facts we have been citing is this: In an ideal situation one should have a personal physician—one who becomes acquainted with one's idiosyncrasies and peculiarities and who continually makes use of this special information. Physicians should not be—exclusively—highly specialized experts in a very limited area. The facts of individuality also draw attention to the desirability of having prescription drugs labeled as to contents; thus one who knows of his susceptibility to some specific drug or antibiotic will be forewarned if labeling is required.

An interesting sidelight on the life of Helen Keller, which bears on drug action, has come to my attention recently. She was, in her first eighteen months of life, a precocious child. At six months of age she could already say a few words, and there was nothing wrong with her sight or hearing. Later came a "mysterious illness" which not only blinded her and took away her hearing but wiped out everything she knew—

practically all memory of words. One word "wah wah" (water) she remembered from the early months when she first began to talk.

According to information obtained indirectly from Helen Keller's first cousin, a physician in Paris, Kentucky, it seems highly probable that her "mysterious illness" (called "acute congestion of the stomach and brain" by the physician who attended her in Alabama) was due to her idiosyncrasy for quinine, which had been given her for malaria.

Idiosyncrasies with respect to quinine are common, and the symptoms associated with Helen Keller's illness—gastrointestinal distress and ultimately the loss of both sight and hearing—are in accord with what is known of quinine poisoning, in which "hearing and vision are particularly disturbed."

While no one will ever know the complete facts, it appears that the calamity which befell Helen Keller when she was almost nineteen months old was due to an unusual susceptibility to quinine poisoning coupled, quite probably, with having received heavy doses.

CHAPTER IX

Sleep, Exercise and Sports

Inborn differences are of such magnitude that all sorts of minor and major calamities—even including insanity and death—can result from accepting the idea that with respect to sleep, exercise and recreation we are all substantially alike.

If one asks a group of college students to register anonymously how much daily sleep they would *like,* the answers may range from three, four or five hours up to eleven or twelve. These estimates are based on the assumption that each student is perfectly free and independent and can adopt any schedule he or she wishes. Medical experience shows that some people have gone for years without more than two or three hours' sleep a night.

Environmentalists attribute such differences merely to *habit* without giving a hint as to how such "habits" got started, or why people "get used to" such widely differing amounts of sleep. Considering the other facts of inborn individuality, it is easy to see that these differences have a biological basis. In view of the large differences in our nervous systems and brains, uniformity could not be expected. That sleep patterns have a biological basis is shown by the sleep behavior of animals. Chickens, for example, are monophasic in their sleep; that is, they fill their daily sleep quota in one stretch. Other animals such as cats (or lions) are polyphasic in that they indulge in a series of "cat naps" during each twenty-four hours. Some animals consistently "go to bed with the chickens" and do all their sleeping at night; some, like cats, are nocturnal and carry on all sorts of interesting activities after dark.

In human beings we see these animal patterns mimicked with variations. Some individuals would never think of taking a daytime nap. Others cannot resist daytime naps if they have a chance. Historically, Napoleon and Edison stand out as individuals who tended to have polyphasic sleep patterns. Both had the reputation of requiring very little sleep but both were prone to take short naps during the day. There are many variations; some tend to go to bed early and perhaps rise early; others are loath to go to bed until the night is at least half gone.

My own case exhibits some peculiarities which are interesting and sometimes disconcerting. I am definitely disinclined to be nocturnal, in the sense of wanting to stay up late in the evening. This disinclination is so strong that I usually do not work at all in the late evenings and I have never, during my college days or since, stayed up to study, read or work past midnight. Whenever I have a deadline to meet I retire early and get up early enough the next morning to do what has to be done. No one suggested this pattern to me; in college almost everyone I knew worked late at night as a matter of course. I found out for myself that late hours were no good for me but that during early hours my efficiency was incomparably better.

I have also found over the years that my make-up is such that I cannot work effectively, uninterrupted by sleep, from daylight till dark. The kind of work which I need to do is often such that if the quality is low, it had better not be done at all, so that I gain nothing by trying to plug away regardless. About five or ten minutes' sleep in the middle of the day has always made a world of difference in the way I feel. I have had to put up with this characteristic all through my adult life.

When I was a junior in college I worked on a road construction gang which operated on a "bonus system"—the amount of our pay was determined by the amount of highway we laid each day. My job was to load a wheelbarrow with gravel, then wheel and dump its contents onto an apron. It took three of us to bring the required amount of gravel and sand for each mix, and the one to get his barrow load onto the apron last had to wheel it over the previous fellow's leavings and dump it on top. If one was *slow*, it made the job for him much harder; hence, because of this as well as the bonus system, there was a continuous race among those hauling gravel and sand to get there early with one's load. This work, at top speed, was tougher than any I had ever done before and in a short time I had a severe headache. When the half-hour noon period came I didn't know whether I could last out the first day. I gobbled down the contents of my lunch bucket and curled up on the side of the road to sleep—a total of about twenty minutes was available—and after this I felt like a new person and was ready for the afternoon's work. Without this rest I would not have been able to make it. I was slight of build, weighed not more than 130 pounds, and the work was such as to tax a much stronger person.

All during my professional career I have tried to avoid one o'clock classes because these would prevent my midday rest. My leanings toward this midday respite have been accentuated by the fact that beginning with my first year of university teaching and my aforementioned ulcer, I have followed the doctor's advice and avoided coffee. I never cared much for coffee, so that has been a small sacrifice. If I drink coffee in the midmorning or at lunch, then I can forgo the midday rest without getting sleepy. Even half a cup at lunchtime will last me until late afternoon, since I am very sensitive to caffeine; then I get sleepy. This, of course, throws me off my preferred schedule. In emergencies I use coffee to make my schedule adjust to that of others.

I suspect that there are millions of people who have the same biological inclination toward the diphasic sleep pattern that I have, and that they overcome this by drinking coffee or else they endure the inconvenience and inefficiency rather than be thought "peculiar." I have attended not a few early afternoon conferences, sometimes involving bigwigs, where it was obvious to me that several of the participants were mentally nodding their heads, whether they were actually doing so or not. On one such occasion the chairman of the meeting actually went to sleep and caused an embarrassing situation.

Diphasic sleepers are probably in the minority, and those who set committee meetings, arrange schedules, etc., are more likely to belong to the monophasic school. If so, they proceed, without the shadow of a question, on the assumption that everyone can adapt to their pattern. They are often oblivious of the existence of those who are constitutionally different. Of course, there are those who are "in between"; they sometimes take a midday rest but it doesn't seem imperative. Whatever one's pattern may be, he expects to find in others the *same pattern*. If the other person's pattern *appears* to be different, it is assumed that he is indulging himself in imaginings that ought to be discarded.

I have myself been guilty of attempting to impose my own sleep rhythm on students. When I first came to the University of Texas, scheduling the first course in biochemistry was difficult. One time of day was available; however, this was eight A.M. This suited me fine because I am at my brightest (least dull) in the early morning hours. I was not aware at this time of the innate differences in people's sleep patterns and assumed that anyone who wanted to learn biochemistry could do so at eight o'clock in the morning as well as at any other time. For the twenty-odd years that I taught this course it was always at eight o'clock. Anyone who would have liked the course at a different hour was out of luck!

There are people, as I have come to find out in recent years, who seem not to be able mentally to get up steam in the early morning. Indeed, some are not at their best until ten or eleven o'clock. I had a research student several years ago whom I never could really get going until about three-thirty in the afternoon. From then on until the late evening he was an excellent worker. Occasionally I have had students who tended, when things got interesting, to work all night. Others may work till early morning and then sleep until noon. I now try to be tolerant and let students, when they get into their own research, set their own hours.

Another peculiarity of my make-up is that I cannot take sleep in large doses. This parallels my inability to be wakefully efficient for long hours during the day. For the last twenty-five years at least I have waked up every night for an hour or so in the middle of the night. According to the supposed authorities, this is one of the three types of insomnia, and a magazine article recently indicates that this is a warning sign of oncoming mental disease. One who believes this warning may indeed become mentally deranged by worrying about it, but fortunately for me I do not regard this as a disease but as a manifestation of my individuality. Insomnia is said to be of three types: some victims can't go to sleep the first part of the night; some cannot sleep after an early morning hour; and some, like myself, can't sleep in the middle of the night.

I do not regard my condition as a disease; if it is, it is an attractive one for me. My mind is clearest during this hour or so and I reserve this time to do my best thinking. I go to bed with problems unsolved, but when I get up in the morning, after having had this quiet hour in the night, the best solution I can devise inevitably comes to me. I ordinarily lie in bed during the hour or so with my eyes closed. If I am going on a trip and need to make a few memoranda, I jot them down in the dark and manage to read them the next day. If I have a careful letter or passage to write, I work out the phrasing during my waking hour and remember it the next day when I write. This has happened thousands of times.

I have no record or memory of just when I started consistently waking up in the middle of the night. It was not, however, until I reached my forties. I do remember, however, that when I was in college an extra-difficult problem in calculus bothered me, but in the night the answer came to me and in the morning I knew it. Also, two specific ideas relating to chemistry and biochemistry came to me in the night in my early professional career and each was published shortly afterward in a scientific journal. It may be that the tendency to have a waking hour (or a semiwaking period) goes back to my early adulthood. This is not important since no one else should expect their sleep pattern to be just like mine.

George Herbert Palmer, a professor of philosophy at Harvard, told students of his pattern, which was like—but unlike—mine. He never during his adult life slept through the night. Usually he would sleep only an hour or two, and then would remain awake a similar period. He learned to lie in bed quiescently and avoided fretting and would be refreshed in the morning. Unlike me he avoided serious thinking. In this respect he was far less fortunate than I am. While I do not *force* myself to do serious thinking, it comes easily when I am in this relaxed state. If I were a philosopher, this would be the time to develop philosophic ideas. Most of what is in this book has been outlined and often phrased during my waking hours in the middle of the night.

That such a sleeping pattern as Professor Palmer's or mine has a physiological basis and is not merely the result of a chance habit is indicated by some experiments carried out many years ago by Professor Nathaniel Kleitman of Chicago, one of the prominent students of sleep. He, with a graduate student, went far back into Mammoth Cave in Kentucky to get away from daylight influences and there they set up quarters and tried to alter their sleep patterns, at the same time keeping track of their body temperatures. Body temperature goes down when we sleep and rises when we are awake.

Kleitman and his student planned to try out working and sleeping on a schedule which would be appropriate for a twenty-eight-hour day—there would be six of such "days" to an ordinary week of 168 hours. The shift was readily made by the student; within a week or so his body temperature was going down *six* times during 168 hours and he slept accordingly—when his body temperature was low. Professor Kleitman on the other hand did not adjust in the same way; his body temperature continued to go down *seven* times during 168 hours. He soon found himself out of phase; he couldn't sleep when he was supposed to on the adjusted schedule because his temperature was high; on the other hand he had great difficulty staying awake when he was supposed to because his temperature was down.

Difference in age was not the basis for the difference, as other studies show. Even newborn babies exhibit different sleep patterns because of innate differences in their body wisdoms—their regulating mechanisms do not work quite the same. The same differences are observed whenever people are forced to change to an artificial rhythm—five hours on and five hours off, in the Navy, for example. Some can adjust readily; others have great difficulty.

Some round-the-world travelers have a continuous battle on their hands when they go from one time belt to another in rapid succession. Like Professor Kleitman, their regulating mechanism shifts very sluggishly. Other travelers, like Kleitman's graduate student, change their sleep schedule from day to day with no great inconvenience.

A striking case of a stubborn mechanism came to my attention in a chance conversation with a prominent fellow scientist. As a student he chose astronomy for his field and became thoroughly trained as an astronomer. After spending all the years—and money—necessary to get a thorough astronomical training, he eventually decided to give up astronomy entirely and enter a new field. Why? Because, as he told me, he could not adjust to the hours that he found an astronomer had to adopt. The combination of observing at night and trying to be a member of a society where the majority of people are awake during the day was too much for him, and at great sacrifice he changed his career. If something had been known about diverse sleep patterns during college days he could have been saved a great deal of unnecessary stress as well as expense. A person with a less rugged make-up, and less common sense, might have been driven to insanity by his inability to live up to what he had expected of himself. Many, I'm sure, have suffered severe mental stress (and doping) because they have unusual sleep patterns and yet have tried to comply with the demands of what they imagine to be normal.

The moral of our discussion about sleep patterns is that everyone ought to find out and adapt to his or her natural pattern if feasible, and we all should be more understanding of others who may be members of a different kind of minority group than we usually think of. If one has a sleep pattern that falls in readily with common convention, then it may require no special attention. If the sleep pattern is unusual, this should not cause worry; worry can contribute toward many diseases, including real insomnia. My own personal inclination is not to tamper artificially with my sleep-regulating mechanism, except in emergencies, either by the use of caffeine, which keeps me awake, or by using sleeping pills, which would make me sleep. If I tamper I am in danger of disrupting a mechanism which if well treated will give me the amount of sleep I need at the time when I need it. Proper nutrition, reasonable exercise and recreation, and the cultivation of wholesome and healthy mental attitudes are all important factors in keeping our sleep-regulating body wisdom (as well as all other body wisdoms) in good working order.

Those who accept implicitly the uniformity idea would probably be willing to accept the statement that everyone needs a certain prescribed amount of exercise every day. From our previous discussions it should be evident that not everyone requires the same amount.

Personally I know from close observation that I cannot work effectively, cannot think up to par, cannot keep in good spirits and sleep properly unless I get exercise equivalent to walking something like an average of four miles a day. This need for a substantial amount of recreational exercise has been with me during my entire adult life. Bertrand Russell, the aged mathematician and philosopher, has said that six miles of walking a day would be more beneficial to unhappy businessmen than any change in philosophy. Actually, in my experience such exercise is enough to change my philosophy —at least my whole outlook on life.

Curiously, I have had to learn this fact of life over and over. I remember an occasion years ago in Oregon when my publishers wanted me to revise a biochemistry book. I agreed and started in on the job. Day after day I went through the necessary motions, but nothing seemed to click. What I wrote didn't sound good to me and I knew it wouldn't to anyone else. Eventually—and this is a *most* unusual thing for me to do—I gave up. I decided I wasn't getting anywhere and that I might as well admit it. I felt badly about it—help-less—but didn't know what to do. After a week or so of this helpless feeling something happened! The weather cleared a bit and I found my way to the golf course a couple of times within a week. This was what I needed, and things began quickly to look up. It had not percolated through to me that for several weeks I had had no recreational exercise. It had been windy, cold and very rainy—not merely the drizzle we were used to—but it was not until I had recovered from my debacle that I realized that this lack of outdoor exercise had gotten me down. A couple of weeks later I felt like tackling the book revision again and went completely through it without a hitch or a doubt.

About this time one of my former students who was com-pleting his doctorate at another institution wrote me, vaguely threatening suicide. On the assumption that he was like myself (which in this case proved right) I urged him to take regular exercise in the gymnasium—this is what I had done during my student days. He followed my advice, snapped out of it, finished his training and has led an outstandingly successful life.

Within a week of this writing I have had a somewhat similar experience. In this case I began rather suddenly to sleep poorly. I had difficulty in going to sleep and in staying asleep. This was unusual for me and I was a bit concerned. I tumbled, however, to the fact that because of a combination of travel and unfavorable weather, I had not been on the golf course for more than three weeks. I immediately called a halt to everything I was doing and got out on a Friday afternoon —an unusual day for me—and played eighteen holes of golf. That night, even though the game had by no means exhausted me, I had no trouble at all going to sleep and my middle-of-the-night period of wakefulness did not come until five A.M.!

In a Harvard study reported in a little book, *What People Are,* Professor C. W. Heath noted that most of the men included in the study felt "logey," dispirited and lacking in energy when they did not get enough exercise, but that *a small group reported no such effects.* This should be conclusive (should it not!) when considered in conjunction with the testimony of a Yale man, Robert Hutchins, who said that he made it a practice when he felt the urge to get out and exercise to lie down and relax until the urge wore off.

Being highly dependent on exercise I am prejudiced in favor of others' being as dependent as I am. But I have to keep telling myself that all people are not built alike. I know that some people can adapt far more readily to a sedentary life than I can. (I am still not completely convinced that it is good for them.) Even among young able-bodied golf players there are those who prefer to ride in carts, whereas others who are older and have a much better excuse for riding prefer to walk.

Physicians are not in agreement on the matter of the

place and importance of exercise; this is in part a reflection of their differing personal tendencies toward a sedentary life; they have among their ranks individuals who badly need regular exercise, and also those who tend to follow the Robert Hutchins' philosophy. Particularly notable is the disagreement as to the best course to follow when heart difficulties arise. I have known men who after a mild heart attack were advised by their physicians never to go near a golf course again; I also know of physicians who strongly advise in such cases a gradual build-up of exercise until the patient is able to walk extensively, or even run. A Cleveland man of sixty-five who had suffered a heart attack built up his exercise capacity until, under expert supervision, he ran ten miles in about seventy minutes!

Such strenuous activity did not work out so well with the novelist Madison Cooper, author of *Sironia, Texas,* who habitually ran a mile or more several times a week to keep fit. Immediately after one of his runs at the age of sixty-two he had a heart attack and died. Tacitly he had accepted the uniformity idea and the false concept that what he was *used to*—running—could do him no harm. He did not recognize his individuality—his lack of adaptability—and it cost him his life.

If one accepts the idea that people are substantially alike, the case of the Cleveland runner demonstrates that running is tolerated well by heart patients. The case of Madison Cooper, however, demonstrates the opposite. There must be something wrong with the underlying assumption of uniformity.

A clue as to how these widely divergent observations can be reconciled was published unobtrusively in a short scientific article recently. Without getting too technical, the problem of just how blood clots and how the various biochemical factors which are involved interact in the complex process has been a muddle for scores of years. One authoritative source indicates that no other part of physiology has been so confused by contradictory findings and interpretations.

When one accepts the idea of biochemical individuality, he sees how this can be. Getting a clear picture of the clotting mechanism *in man* would be like getting a clear picture of the branching of arteries from the aortic arch *in man*. *It cannot be done.* It should be possible to get a clear picture of the mechanism and the various factors that enter into the coagulation of *my* blood or of *yours,* but when one tries to include all human bloods, the picture gets confused. The blood chemistries of individuals vary—not just in trifling ways—enough to make a picture which is accurate for one individual, inaccurate for another.

The clotting of blood is, of course, intimately concerned with coronary heart attacks and also with "strokes" because in each case unwanted clotting causes stoppage of blood vessels. What Dr. T. P. Bond of the Medical School at Galveston found and published recently is that exercise affects the clotting mechanisms of individuals *un*uniformly. In some individuals exercise may cause the release into the blood of factors which make the blood clot less readily, whereas in others, exercise causes the release of clot-promoting factors. If these observations hold up, exercise should be *discouraged* in those whose blood clots more readily as a result of it, whereas exercise should be *encouraged* in those whose blood clots less readily as a result of the exertion. So doctors on both sides of the fence may be right—*in appropriate cases.*

My intuition tells me that the situation will not prove quite this simple, but it also tells me most emphatically that the relationships between exercise and blood clotting will never clear up as long as the scientists who investigate the problem adhere tenaciously to the uniformity idea.

Do people, when they do "what comes naturally," differ substantially in their tendency to exercise? The answer based on observation and animal experimentation is an emphatic "Yes." In our laboratories, for example, we selected a group of young rats of uniform age, which had been subjected to the same environmental influences, and studied their individual tendencies to exercise. Each was in a separate cage to which was attached an "exercise wheel" where each rat could go to play as much as desired. Every revolution of the wheel in either direction was automatically counted. In a group of nineteen of these rats which *looked* as much alike as twin brothers (no runts) we found tremendous divergence. While every rat tended to spin the wheel, the "laziest" one spun it to travel *on the average* 158 feet per day, whereas the most active rat in the group traveled *on the average* nearly six miles per day—about two hundred times as far as his lazy friend!

Those who have observed children know that they also show relative differences in their activity. Some are always on the go; others tend to be far less active. It would be surprising indeed if this were not so—if individuality in this regard were to be found in rats, but not in human beings.

Are relatively inactive children completely healthy and should they be encouraged (and even coerced) to get out and play? While I recognize innate differences in tendencies to be active, I think physical inactivity, in a child particularly, is probably a sign of lack of vigor and health. If such a child is induced (preferably with adroitness) to go outside to play, he may eat better, and if he is then furnished the kind of wholesome food that is needed, his spontaneous activity may be increased. Forced play is, of course, of dubious value. In a recent study involving rats, it was found that even among these lowly creatures, giving them an opportunity to play (in an exercise wheel) improved their mental ability in the solution of maze problems, but that forced exercise did not have the same effect.

In primitive nature there was often an inducement to exercise—to escape from enemies, procure food. It is doubtful if we will ever get away from our biological background sufficiently so that rocking-chair exercise will be enough to stir up our blood and make us vibrant with health. I decry the fact that walking has gone out of fashion to the extent that in many localities there are no sidewalks or other decent places to walk. A young man who sentimentally frequents "the street where she lives" is liable to get hit by a passing automobile. Thomas Jefferson, who lived to be eighty-three (without the help of antibiotics), was a strong advocate of walking and condemned the use of horses for transporting people. Paul Dudley White, the famous heart specialist, practices what he preaches when he rides a bicycle when reasonable opportunities arise. Alonzo Stagg at ninety-eight still used a hand-operated lawn mower, and Roscoe Pound, who wrote a five-volume work on American law after he was eighty-six, was a devotee of walking and bicycling.

Everyone who neglects recreational exercise misses, according to my admittedly prejudiced view, something important and extremely beneficial. But I do not accept the idea that people's needs are the same with respect to exercise. People are built differently, and it is possible that these differences are even greater with respect to exercise than I have suggested.

Recreation of every kind, whether it involves physical exercise or not, is something which must be tailored to fit the individual concerned. I have already let the secret out that I enjoy golf—also card playing. I have friends, however, who have no use whatever for either of these activities, and they still remain my friends. Others like golf but no cards; others like cards but no golf.

One reason why there are many games and kinds of games—there ought to be more—is so that many different people with different make-ups can enjoy them. Haven't you heard it jokingly said, "Can't a game be invented so *I* can win?" Because we are constitutionally so different from one another, our capabilities are distinctive; some select one game and others select others. There are those whose constitutions make being a baseball fan very easy; for others the game may move too slowly—or perhaps it is the peanuts they don't like.

There is, of course, no such thing as the best game. Games, like so many other things in life, are a matter of individual choice, and these choices are based not only on upbringing and training but also on constitutional differences. A really competent player of any game must have a suitable natural endowment to build on; practice makes perfect and everyone is entitled to try, but not everyone who tries will become outstanding.

Eyesight characteristics, musculature differences, physiological endurance characteristics enter into the make-up of every kind of athlete. Coaches and trainers may like to think that they have contributed a great deal to an athlete's progress, but many of them at least recognize that the inborn characteristics of the individual person play a tremendous role. An experienced and successful coach never tries to make a pitcher of a player who doesn't have a pitching arm, or a quarterback out of a less agile fellow who might be an excellent guard.

I remember several years ago we had on our football team in Texas a player who was a phenomenally accurate passer but still didn't click. After watching his performance I became convinced that he was relatively deficient in peripheral vision ("normal" people do differ enormously in this respect), because he would often get smothered by a tackler coming from the side that he should have seen and avoided. He was like a horse with blinders on. One of the highly important factors which makes for an outstanding quarter-back (and for other players, too) is a pair of eyes that can see peripherally—have no blind side—and can judge the speed of players or objects from all angles with accuracy. Without this kind of eyes, muscular coordination and speed are liable to be of little value in games such as football, basketball, hockey, etc. Inborn individuality with respect to eyesight is, of course, not a revolutionary idea, but it extends further than we sometimes think.

Individuality with respect to muscles and their functioning is just as distinctive as that of eyesight. A successful track coach knows that he can't make a sprinter out of a miler, or vice versa, and that to excel at a high jump doesn't make one a good hurdler or shot putter or swimmer. He also knows, of course, that there are some athletes who are versatile and can do relatively well in a number of events. Training in this case helps, but the inborn characteristics must be there at the start if there is to be excellence.

Tragedy can happen in sports too when the idea that young men are substantially alike is accepted. A few years ago we had on two different campuses in Texas deaths of football players who suffered from heat stroke. It is no secret that in the major part of Texas we have *hot* weather for several months of the year. During early fall workouts the players encountered this, and the tacit assumption was made that young men in good physical condition could all stand about the same treatment, so they were all put through their paces.

What has often been overlooked is that healthy young men do not have the same body temperatures at rest, and that exercise will not affect temperatures to the same extent in all individuals. The Harvard study by C. W. Heath showed that young men have initial temperatures ranging from 97° to 100° and that only about eighteen per cent have the "normal" temperature, 98.6°. Roger Bannister, who first ran a mile in under four minutes, is now a physiologist in England. In a report now six years old he gave the results obtained when he had three athletes exercise vigorously to the same extent (running uphill on a treadmill) in what was considered a warm environment (about 80°). Vigorous exercise always causes one's body temperature to rise. In two athletes the temperatures went up less than four degrees while in one athlete it rose nearly seven degrees up to 104.7°. If Bannister had tested a larger group—the size of a football squad, for example—the range would have been wider, and some one or two would certainly have had temperatures substantially above 104.7°. Now transfer the locale of such a squad to Texas on a hot day—perhaps close to 100° in the shade and much hotter in the sun—and it is not hard to imagine what could happen. It did, and two young men lost their lives.

Outside the field of athletics a tremendous number of discomforts, distresses and unnecessary strifes are caused by people having very different reactions to temperature. These begin when we are newborn babies, as we have already seen. It is often assumed by any one of us who happens to like a warm (or cool) room or warm (or cool) weather, that anyone else can become accustomed to what *we* like. If they don't adapt, there is something wrong with them. Of course, there is such a thing as acclimatization, but the facts of physiological individuality tell us that some will adapt far more readily than others. Some individuals are so built that they will continuously like warm weather and dislike cold. Others may have the opposite reactions consistently. I know of Texas residents of long standing who look forward every year to the hot summers; I know others who think the winters are fine but hate the summers.

When we have had desirable men under consideration for faculty positions at the University of Texas, I have always thought it important to know how they react to warm weather. If they react unfavorably they are likely not to stay. This was an especially important matter before air conditioning became common. Of course, there are bound to be complainers and malingerers in any human population. The truth is—and I believe truth will not hurt us in the end—that people because of inborn differences adapt very differently to various climatic conditions.

Why, in the realm of sports and elsewhere, do individuals have "off" and "on" days? It is well known that baseball pitchers, for example, sometimes have lots of "stuff," yet at other times have, by comparison, almost nothing. The same holds true in football, baseketball, tennis, bowling, golf, running, jumping and other sports. Typists, salesmen, preachers, housewives, teachers and others have their off days too but they often cannot be judged objectively.

When there are marked differences in performance, there must be physiological reasons back of these differences. These may rest upon psychology or on such physiological variables as sleep, exercise, temperature and climatic conditions and—possibly most important—nutrition. No blanket reason can be found, and only when we reject the uniformity idea and get down to cases can we hope to make progress. Each individual has his own set of reasons for being "off" on a given occasion.

There are among athletes those who have peculiarities in sleep patterns, differences in reactions to temperatures, differences in reactions to foods. Mild food "allergies" are very common, according to some authorities, and these could be responsible for individuals' being out of sorts. When a baby cries, we immediately think of food. Do people ever cease to be like babies in this respect?

If I were a team manager I would want to know about my players' peculiarities so that suitable adjustments could be made. It is entirely possible that a midday nap would do wonders for some athletes, but you can be sure it wouldn't work for all. Unfortunately, the idea of uniformity has been so widely held that people are loath to admit they are different. In the case of top athletes, however, such an admission would probably be socially permissible.

CHAPTER X

What About a "Science of Man"?

It is a truism that life presents many apparent contradictions. We must recognize and face these seeming paradoxes if we are to attempt to apply science to the social world around us.

We have noted that individuals sometimes rebel at the rules of society and that these rules and customs to be effective must not neglect the individuality of the people who are to live by them. This tendency to rebel should not suggest that individuals have no use for society. The sociologists are right when they emphasize our dependence on each other, and upon the society in which we live.

The fact that there have been independent souls like Thoreau, who seemed to succeed in withdrawing from society—to a degree—or the fact that each of us may be in the mood at times to "let the rest of the world go by," should not blind us to the fact that human beings in general, and most of the time, need each other—even desperately. An individual cannot be described or understood, nor can he live his life, isolated from the society of which he is a part.

We are greatly influenced by what our neighbors, near and far, think of us. It is for this reason that if we are conspicuously different—have a harelip, bald head, a birthmark, a peculiar quirk of mind or an unusual taste—we tend to want to hide what we regard as a blemish. We want to be identified with the mainland of humanity and not be as an island.

These two seemingly paradoxical but complementary facts must be incorporated into our thinking: *individuals need society; society needs individuals.* That people need society has perhaps been emphasized enough by sociologists; that society cannot get along without individuals has been in the shadows because of general lack of knowledge about the dimensions and scope of individuality.

While differentness may at times appear to be inconvenient, it is, generally speaking, neither a liability to the person who is different nor to the society which is made up of such persons—certainly differentness is not a liability if it is faced with candor and understanding. Frank Moore Colby, editor and essayist of two generations back, wrote, thinking of politics and business: "A lopsided man runs the fastest along the little side hills of success." If we were to eliminate from history all those who were a little bit lopsided or eccentric, there would be little left to record. Orville Wright emphasized the importance of differentness in the realm of thinking when he said, "If we all worked on the assumption that what is accepted as true is really true, there would be little hope of advance."

Even those who have some conspicuous unattractive difference need not, because of it, become rejected or useless to society. It is gratifying to see Jimmy Durante turn a real blemish—his snozzle—into a valuable trademark that helps him sell his talents.

My own personal experiences with differentnesses show that they very often turn up on the credit side of the ledger. The ideas set forth in this book had their inception in the differentness I exhibited when I was administered morphine. More important than this one incident, so far as the development of these ideas is concerned, is a "blemish" I have had to learn to live with—namely, a severe limitation in my eyesight with respect to reading.

For one thing I am afflicted with *aniseikonia,* a little-known condition discovered about thirty years ago at the Dartmouth Eye Institute. It appears to involve the production of images of different sizes and shapes on the two retinas. It is not necessarily rare. Whether this is my whole difficulty I do not know, but the eyesight trouble has been with me since before I completed my formal education. Even during my college days I used to be most envious of one of my close friends who could read and study all night without discomfort, while I never could read for long periods with any pleasure. He was very near-sighted—another "blemish" which can work greatly to one's advantage if he is to do extensive book work. This friend in turn envied me in that I had very acute vision (this is characteristic of those who have aniseikonia) and had no difficulty in recognizing people a long way off. I have been to numerous doctors, have tried all kinds of eye exercises, have had an operation on my eye muscles, tried reading with one eye at a time, have been fitted with aniseikonic glasses—all without altering substantially the strain caused by prolonged reading. I can see well, but reading for more than a half hour at a time is like dragging a log up a hillside.

My inability to read extensively has been a severe handicap in my professional work. When someone starts to question "Have you read . . .?" I can almost answer "No" before they complete the query. This is sometimes embarrassing. I have missed much and continue to miss a great deal because I cannot read more.

On the other hand, this differentness—my inability to pore over books—has been a tremendous factor in my developing ideas that would never have come to me had I been a prodigious reader. Much of the time that might have been spent reading in the library or at home, getting acquainted with "what is accepted as true," was spent in *thinking* on my own. Because I was not steeped in the traditional attitudes (brainwashed), this thinking took directions that were *different*. It was easy to avoid the difficulty of getting my mind so cluttered up with odds and ends of second-hand lumber—a random selection of the writings of the past—that I had no room to build any ideas of my own.

This differentness has greatly influenced my scientific activities throughout my life. Because of it, it was natural that I selected for study and research things that were far enough from the beaten trails so that I did not have to follow, in the library, the work of a multitude of others in order to be abreast of current progress. As soon as a subject I was working on became of general interest, I tended to turn in new directions. When the vitamin I discovered—pantothenic acid—became widely known and scores of articles concerning it began to be published each year, I left it for the field of biochemical individuality, which I had largely to myself for a number of years. My productivity would have been far more restricted and less significant if I had been endowed with "normal" eyesight.

Our dependence on culture rests upon the prior existence of *individuals* who possessed differentness in the form of peculiar gifts. How barren our culture would be for me per-

sonally if there had not been composers who wrote the op-
eratic and other songs I love—songs I couldn't possibly write
—and were there not individual musicians who can sing
them in a way that I could not learn to do! What a complete
blank literary culture would be for me if it were not for the
individual talents of Shakespeare, Victor Hugo, Tolstoy,
Galsworthy, George Eliot, Theodore Dreiser and others who
wrote books I could not possibly write. Possibly if I had read
more widely, the less worthy material would have diluted
out what has meant so much to me.

I remember on two particular occasions when I have
been thrilled—goose pimples and all—by pieces of sculpture
and architecture created by *individuals* with unusual gifts.
Once as I entered the Art Institute building in Chicago,
which I had done many times before, I encountered something new, two contrasting pieces of statuary—one on either
side of the hall—one of Voltaire, the other of Joan of Arc. I
have no idea who the sculptors were—names don't stick with
me well and often don't matter—but the artistic effect of
these two pieces facing each other gave me a thrill that I can
never forget. I came back years later, hoping to see it over
again, but the attendant knew nothing about the where-
abouts of the pieces of sculpture. He only worked there. At
another time I was walking toward the main part of the Yale
University campus when suddenly a group of buildings more
magnificent than any I had ever seen came into view. The
group and the setting were of such exquisite beauty and impressed me so much that a few years later I made a special
stop at New Haven, again hoping to capture the view. I did
not succeed. Handsome buildings were there but new ones
had been added, and the particular grouping that had impressed me as being so spectacular could not be located.

Such pieces of art are produced by individuals, and their
appreciation by others is individual. We make artistic and

literary friends *in spots,* as we do our other friends. What some critic or group of critics think about a painting, sculpture or literary production means little to me if I like it. A group of critics cannot think collectively; they cannot come up with anything that surpasses the individual reactions of each one; neither can a committee of gifted writers get their heads together and write a supermasterpiece. Of course, on a statistical basis if many critics like something it will probably be liked by many others.

The need that society has for individuals is most real; it encompasses every part of life and will continue as long as society lasts. There are thousands of kinds of day-to-day jobs as well as more inspiring ones that need to be done, and a multitude of special gifts must be possessed by *individuals* if these jobs are to be done well and the work is to be enjoyed as it should be.

That the need of society for individuals has not been appreciated by many who have tried to develop a "science of man" is fully evident. I welcomed years ago a single compact book which set forth the position of the current "social scientists" in as authoritative a manner as could be wished. It was called *The Proper Study of Mankind,* written by an able writer, Stuart Chase, at the instigation of leaders in the Social Science Research Council and the Carnegie Corporation. About eighty leaders in the social science field cooperated with the author.

It is most surprising that there was expressed in this book such a passionate interest in the "dirty-gray man" referred to in the first chapter of this book. Chase says, "Social systems which endure *are built on the average person,* who can be trained to occupy *any* position adequately if not brilliantly." (The italics are his.) At another point, he indicates how administrators (political leaders) must be able to recite the "universals" backward in their sleep: "This is what all men, everywhere, since time out of mind, under such and such conditions, are prone to do." He even gives the average man a name, George Rutherford Adams, and describes him as living in *Middleburg;* he is about five feet nine inches tall, weighs 158 pounds, is thirty-one years old, goes to church about the average number of times a year, has about an average income and about the average number of children for a man of his age.

It is pathetic that Chase and his numerous associates thought to build social science on the concept of George Rutherford Adams. He goes on in his book to ask and answer questions about him. "What kind of being is George Rutherford Adams? What shaped him? How did he get to be what he is? We know that he is the product of a group and the culture that goes with it." Evidently the idea of the Marxist Bukharin, that people are stuffed with environmental influences like a sausage is stuffed with meat, is quite satisfactory—or was—to the social scientists who approved of Chase's book.

There is not one word about George Rutherford Adams' heredity and it is to be presumed that this had nothing whatever to do with his being what he was. What a gross neglect of the facts of biology! Dr. Walter Alvarez, the famous Mayo physician, in 1958 leveled the same criticism on "most of the present-day books on psychiatry" in which "there is not even a short section on heredity. The book resembles a text on paleontology written for a fundamentalist college with not one word on evolution."

It should cause no surprise that a social science built on the average man, George Rutherford Adams, should not be successful, because the concept is based on fundamental error. Logically, George Rutherford Adams' heart would have average pumping capacity; all of his organs including his endocrine glands would be average; he would have the average amount of hair on his head, parted in the *middle,* and he would have average acuity in every facet of his mind. No one person has all these "averages" in his make-up and no composite hypothetical person enters in our society. *All members of society are individuals.*

Social science built on the average man would be like United States geography built upon the concept of the "average state": It has an area of 72,000 square miles and a population of over 3.5 million. It has about 1,200 square miles of fresh water lakes and 37 square miles of salt lake. Its highest mountains are about 6,000 feet high. About 5,000 square miles of it lie in the Arctic regions, where the ground is frozen the year round (permafrost). It has a shoreline of about 150 miles. The average state produces yearly about ½ million barrels of oil; 300,000 tons of coal; 50,000 pounds of copper; 10 million bushels of wheat; 3 million pounds of tobacco; 1 million bales of cotton; about 150,000 tons of citrus fruit and 9,000 tons of pineapples.

One of the most pervasive and pernicious ideas that is entertained by people today is that people are simply molded to be what they are by their environment. According to this idea, there is such a thing as an average or typical American; for example, one who has been molded to be what he is by the American culture (or lack of it). According to this idea there is also a typical or average Frenchman, Scandinavian or Chinaman, each molded by his respective culture. These typical people, it is supposed, are the ones with whom we are concerned when we deal with Americans, Frenchmen, Scandinavians or Chinese.

To appreciate how ridiculous this idea is, let us imagine, for example, a bookcase or a library full of books, and think of the dilemma we would be in if we were asked (under penalty of death to make it more interesting) to select a typical or average book!

Careful thinking through the problem would bring us to the conclusion that such words as *average, typical* or *normal* have meaning only when one can answer the question: *average, typical* or *normal with respect to what?* If we were asked to pick out a book average or typical with respect to thickness, *or* print size, *or* paper thickness, *or* number of words, *or* number of chapters, *or* number of paragraphs, *or* size of index, we would have relatively little difficulty. But if we were required to pick out a book that was typical in *all* these respects, as well as having typical subject matter treated with typical literary skill, we would be really stumped. Such a book doesn't exist, and if it did it would be a most extraordinary book (in a most uninteresting way) and not a *typical* book at all.

No one cares a whit about an average or typical book, no one ever mentions it, librarians know nothing about it, and no one of them would be willing to institute a search for it. Is "library science" concerned with how average books are to be handled? No, it is concerned with sorting, making available and finding out what is in *individual* books—each one different from all the others.

Why is it that we are relatively well acquainted with books—we treat them individually and never speak of typical or average books? Why, in contrast, are we so ignorant about people? We often speak of the average American, the typical Frenchman, the typical teen-ager, the average housewife, the average five-year old, the average newspaper reader, the typical businessman.

The best answer I can think of to the question of why we are and have been so ignorant about people involves the poet Alexander Pope. Possibly he is merely a scapegoat and it is only in a half-serious mood that I lay the blame on him. In his famous "Essay on Man" is to be found the much quoted line, "The proper study of mankind is man." This is beautifully phrased, but it carries with it—to me—the unmistakable implication that what humanity needs to understand is George Rutherford Adams, the average man. It contains the grandiose idea that if we could understand this "man," all would be well. The proper study of books is not *book* but *books*. The proper study of mankind is not *man* but *men*.

This idea that *man* should be the center of interest, whether it should be traced to Alexander Pope or not, has had a powerful effect on people's thinking. It has been *assumed* that it was valid without serious critical thought. It is one of those ideas that, quoting Orville Wright, "is accepted as true." It isn't. We can get nowhere in our study of books or of human beings by seeking out and concentrating upon the average or typical specimen.

Those who emphasize the effects of culture to the exclusion of hereditary differences would seem to clinch their argument by saying that if a group of one hundred babies of foreign ancestry were to be adopted into American homes, they would become Americans in every sense, and if their facial features did not give them away, they would be *indistinguishable from native-born Americans*.

One could not argue with this statement of fact but it does not prove that heredity is unimportant. Let us look at this problem more closely. When a hundred babies of *American* descent are reared in an American culture, what happens to *them?* As they mature they individually select from their cultural surroundings (which offer a rich choice) those things that fit their own individual selves; in their youth they may also endure other things that are distasteful (music lessons and spinach may be examples), because of parental or other pressure. They never lose their individuality and their distinctive tastes, as the Utopia game shows. Their only alternatives, however, are to accept the culture in which they reside, or else move to a new location. This latter often happens as they become independent and on their own.

If a hundred foreign babies were adopted into American homes, exactly the same thing would happen to them. They would be forced to accept what our culture had to offer—language, dress, customs, schooling—but they would never cease to be individuals. If such a group when they reached high school age were to play the Utopia game, they would show just as wide variability in the items selected as the native-born Americans. The culture in which one lives is an important determinant with respect to language and dress and also with respect to many opinions and ideas, but it does not—cannot—rob one of his biological and psychological individuality. Culture fails in many, many important ways to make us uniform. Our own individual equipment, which we get from our heredity, is of the utmost importance to us individually and to the society in which we live.

One of the underlying reasons why "man" is of great interest to academic people—more so than to those who deal in a more practical way with people—is the desire to develop *generalizations*. This, to many, is the equivalent of developing a science. Students of society have tended to envy the physical, chemical and biological sciences because of the marvelous progress that has been made in these areas. These sciences have been eminently successful in establishing generalizations; it is but natural that social science should emulate them, and try also to develop generalizations. What generalization could be more attractive as a starter than *"All men are alike."* It *seems* to be in line with the Declaration of Independence, and to foster brotherhood.

Stuart Chase has in a later book, *Guides to Straight Thinking,* given a strong clue as to why social scientists have fallen into this fundamental and serious error. Chase, who is a writer and thinker to be admired, discusses thirteen common thinking fallacies. Number one on his list is *overgeneralizing*. Concerning this, he says: "Yet all of us, including the most polished eggheads, are constantly falling into this mental man-trap. It is the commonest, probably the most seductive, and potentially the most dangerous, of all the fallacies." Later in the chapter he says: "We *must* generalize to communicate and to live. But we should beware of beating the gun; of not waiting until enough facts are in to say something useful."

It is exactly this man-trap that has caught those who have tried to build social science or a science of man on George Rutherford Adams, the average man. They have beaten the gun, have not waited until the facts of individuality are in, but have forged ahead—polished eggheads and all—attempting to build a social science on the false overgeneralization that people are substantially all alike.

I am sure that among the sociologists, social anthropologists and social psychologists who appear to adopt this false overgeneralization, there is an increasing number who are now willing to bow, at least slightly, to biology. I have no animus whatever even toward those who do not. I have no inclination to call names. I find it impossible, however, to believe that Stuart Chase or any other intelligent person holds the opinion that *every* child—including Mozart, Shakespeare and Leonardo da Vinci—was originally a George Rutherford Adams and that each was molded by his environment to be somebody else. Almost everyone is willing to accord inborn individuality to the geniuses. But this is not enough. The scientific facts tell us that the world is more democratic than this. *Everyone has inborn individuality.* This is a fact that no true social science can forget.

If social scientists wanted to be truly scientific they should have gone back to Francis Bacon, who believed that things should be looked at first, before attempting generalizations. If human beings had been carefully looked at individually—without preconceived notions about them—the generalization that "all men are alike" would never have been assumed to be true.

What about social science or a science of man? Does it have a future and can it have a future without the generalization "all men are alike"? No one should be so foolish as to catalog all the things that cannot be done in the social science field. One thing is sure: what is needed is not a more and more refined picture of the average man.

There seems to be some parallel between a science of man and library science. One of the objectives of library science is to learn how to sort books; one of the objectives of social science is to learn how to sort people. Imagine how much benefit would come to humanity if it were possible for every child to find his place in the world—a place where he or she could be productive and enjoy his or her work. One of the functions of library science is to make it possible for people to get out of books what is in them. A corresponding function of social science is to make possible getting out of people the good that is in them.

Of course, there is such a thing as prediction, based upon statistics, and one would be rash to place limits on what can be done in this direction. We can now predict with considerable success how many people will die, how many will be born and how many will go to college. Such predictions never deal with individual cases and are not based upon a profound knowledge of the underlying causes, but rather upon specific past experience.

It is certain that statistical methods will be of increasing value in the study of human beings. It is equally certain that these methods cannot serve if they are used merely to conceal individuality. No one is wise enough to know in advance what numerous directions social science or the science of man may take. We should be wise enough to know that such developments must rest on a recognition of the facts of individuality.

It would not be fair to sociologists and to social anthropologists to overgeneralize by suggesting that they are all unrealistic and think primarily in terms of the hypothetical nonexistent average man. One of the most severe critics of this line of thought has been a sociologist, Professor George A. Lundberg of the University of Washington. He was president of the American Sociological Society in 1943. Knowing of my interest in individuality he sent me a copy of an address given to the Sociological Research Society in 1952 in which he went so far as to conclude that because sociologists are not facing problems squarely they "are not taken very seriously in the councils of local community, state and nation. They don't deserve to be taken seriously." It is a tribute to our educational system that men of his opinion are allowed to speak out.

CHAPTER XI

What Will Happen to Psychology and Psychiatry?

We can in one sentence summarize the future of psychology and psychiatry in the new and different world where everyone is recognized as having a high degree of inborn individuality. *Psychology and psychiatry will expand and become far more useful and expert through centering attention on real individuals.* Insofar as psychology's interest has been in George Rutherford Adams, the average man, the tail has been wagging the dog. Eventually "differential psychology" with all of its ramifications will be the dog, wagging the rest of psychology as an appendage.

This comparison is imperfect, however, and does not quite do justice to the situation. There are many complications which must be discussed before we can get a picture of the remarkable developments that are in store in these areas.

For many centuries there has been an interest in the working of people's minds and particularly the fact that some people on occasion generate what appear to be such peculiar ideas, attitudes and interests. Why does not everyone pursue a right-minded and sensible course?

Astrologists sought to solve this problem by ascribing differences of this sort to the influences of the stars and the constellations. We have a remnant of this in the "horoscopes" that are printed in newspapers, but informed people pay little attention to these for the simple reason that people who are born at the same time and hence should be affected by the stars in the same way, turn out often to be vastly different mentally and in every other way from one another.

Phrenology, which considers the contours of people's skulls, was in vogue for several decades as a means of explaining the vagaries of people's minds. The proponents were supposed to be able to tell by feeling the bumps on one's head the person's characteristics and potentialities. This doesn't work out and has been largely discarded.

Francis Galton, a cousin of Charles Darwin, explained people's mental differences on the basis of their heredity. If there was something askew in people's minds, there must be something askew in their heredity. He founded *eugenics,* which is based on the idea that good breeding will produce good bodies and good minds and that the human race can be greatly improved by selective breeding.

Eugenics doesn't work out as simply as this, from the scientific point of view, as we shall discuss later in this chapter. One crucial problem arises in connection with improving the race: In *what ways* should the race be improved and who decides? From the point of view of morals and the life of the family, eugenics is repugnant to many. In addition, it has seemed to smack of determinism and the idea that people are powerless to do anything about the molding of their own lives. Galtonism is largely defunct, though it contains an element of truth which need not be discarded.

Next on the scene came Freud, who was to have a most profound effect on psychology and psychiatry. His fundamental idea was that early events in a child's life, working through the unconscious, are responsible for aberrations, and that the proper treatment for mental illness is "psychoanalysis"—exploring and attempting to understand the significance of these early events. If this is done, according to the Freudian theory, mental health should return. This idea, which carries with it the assumption that babies are essentially uniform until acted upon by their environment, has been embraced by both clinical psychologists and psychiatrists and has had a wide influence. I was told a few years ago by a leading psychiatrist in a large Eastern city that no one could become head of a psychiatry department in a first-rate medical school unless he is a Freudian. This may not be true now.

Closely related to Freudian concepts was the discovery over fifty years ago of *conditioned reflexes* by the famous Russian physiologist, Pavlov. He found that dogs which became accustomed to having a dinner bell sounded at meal-time had become "conditioned" so that they would salivate at the sound of the bell in the absence of food. This "conditioning" fitted in well with Freudian ideas and was a crucial basis for the closely related behavioristic psychology. Watson, a leader in this school, believed that young infants have only two things to which they innately react with fear: one is a loud noise, the other is falling—a feeling of lack of support. He contended that all other fears which older people have arise from these two fundamental ones, by "conditioning." If, for example, an infant falls and bumps his head often enough to associate the falling with the bumping, then he may fear the bumping. If something he has *learned* to fear becomes associated with darkness, then he may fear the dark.

Although Freudianism has been widely accepted by many psychiatrists, it has very little to do with modern medicine. It was founded in its essentials in the 1890's. This was before anything was known about enzymes, genes, hormones or vitamins; in fact, none of these terms was in use at this time. The use of X-rays had not yet been developed.

Freud had a brilliant mind, but his contributions need to be judged in a proper setting. He himself saw the limitations that existed during his lifetime and was more open-minded and less resistant to change than many of his modern followers. Toward the end of his career he wrote: "I can say that I have made many suggestions. Something will come of them in the future. But I cannot tell myself whether it will be much or little."

He knew that the future might bring entirely new developments. He was aware that biological answers might be potent, in fact, he wrote: "They may be the kind which will blow away the whole of our artificial structure of hypotheses." He even foresaw the importance of biochemistry in connection with mental disease. He wrote: "The future may teach us how to exercise a direct influence, by means of particular chemical substances, upon the amounts of energy and their distribution in the apparatus of the mind. It may be that there are other undreamed-of possibilities of therapy. But for the moment we have nothing better at our disposal than the technique of psychoanalysis, and for that reason, in spite of its limitations, it is not to be despised." How prophetic he was and how well he knew that he was looking at the problem of mental disease through a tiny crack in the door!

It seems perfectly clear now for the first time that mental quirks and aberrations must be related to the fact that each individual is highly unique in his entire make-up, including his nervous system and brain. While early events in childhood may play a role—even an important role—in producing aberrations in later life, this must be only a part of the picture. Inborn individuality must play a highly significant role.

That each individual presents a unique problem was one of the basic tenets of Adolf Meyer, of Johns Hopkins University, considered by many to be the dean of American psychiatrists. He remained open-minded; he did not build his psychiatry on any particular theoretical framework, but on the observable facts, regardless of whether these lay in the fields of anatomy, physiology or psychology. He retired over twenty years ago; hence he could not have been acquainted with the numerous evidences of biological individuality which have accumulated in the past two decades. I have a strong feeling that were he alive today he would accept the facts presented in this book with a high degree of interest and enthusiasm.

Psychologists in increasing numbers are becoming aware of the tremendous importance of biological factors. One of these psychologists is Professor Jerry Hirsch of the University of Illinois, who in a lead article in *Science* recently called attention to the regrettable fact that "the 'opinion makers' of two generations literally excommunicated heredity from the behavioral sciences."

If the behavioristic psychologists who founded their approach on Pavlov's "conditioned reflexes" would read Pavlov's writings in the original or in translation, they would find that he did not by any means neglect heredity. In his study of dogs and their conditioning he found four types of dogs: (1) excitable, (2) inhibitory, (3) equilibrated and (4) active. Besides these there were intermediate types. He recognized many inborn differences in the dogs and paid a great deal of attention to them. He would have ridiculed the statement of Watson the behaviorist, who said he could take any one of a dozen healthy infants picked at random and train him, by conditioning, to be *anything* he chose—gifted artist, musician or what not—simply by providing him with a suitable environment. Watson was an out-and-out environmentalist. He said "there is no such thing as inheritance of capacity, talent, temperament, mental constitution and characteristics." Pavlov, who received the Nobel Prize in 1904 for his work on digestion (in dogs), knew that dogs innately react very differently to "conditioning" and he certainly would have inferred that this also applies to human beings.

Before we discuss heredity, which we must do to clarify the present state of affairs in psychology and the future prospects, we should note that the idea of inborn individuality as it applies to psychology and every facet of life is really a very old idea.

On a recent trip to India I had an opportunity to learn something of Ayurvedic medicine, which is indigenous to that country and has centers of activity in Baroda, Bombay and elsewhere. In a translation of Sanscrit writings (Charaka) estimated to be at least 5,000 years old, we find this: "The individual constitution [Prakriti] is an inherited condition that cannot be altered fundamentally. It is a lifelong concern for every individual. This factor of individual personality is of supreme significance in determining the conditions of health and disease in man." It would be too much to expect of these ancient writers that they would in a short statement strike a proper balance between heredity and the ability we have to direct our own lives, but their intuition was remarkable. They saw a part of the picture that the opinion makers of the Western world have excommunicated from their thinking for the past two generations.

The study of heredity is entitled to a prominent place in behavioral science and its excommunication has been most unfortunate. At the present time it is undergoing very rapid development, and this development is accompanied by an understandable amount of confusion and uncertainty as well as overoptimism. Since this perplexity arises particularly in the more common sense and workaday aspects of heredity, it is very pertinent to the future of psychology and psychiatry.

Tremendous strides have been made in recent years in the understanding of the mechanisms of action of desoxyribonucleic acid (*DNA*) molecules, which are fundamental carriers of inheritance. The picture of how inheritance in single-celled organisms takes place is highly complicated but is getting clearer month by month. In these organisms the production of new individuals involves the generation of new single cells *similar to the cells from which they arise.* In a multicellular organism such as a human being—containing hundreds of different kinds of cells (pages 130, 131) and a total of many trillions of them, all in one coordinated parcel —inheritance is far more complicated. It also involves the *DNA's*—there are millions of kinds of these—but *also* other factors of as yet unknown nature. These unknown factors which control the process of "differentiation" make it possible for "like cells to beget *un*like." During the process of differentiation we do, in the cellular realm, gather "figs from thistles." The different types of cells pictured on pages 130, 131 and many more, regularly arise in embryonic life from cell division starting with a single globular cell which appears superficially to be simple. It obviously is not simple, because such a cell is capable of developing into an entire human being. It appears by no means simple now that we can view it by electron microscopy; it contains *many* complicated internal structures. It seems probable that the unknown factors which make possible the production of many different kinds of cells from this one are of great importance in human heredity.

Many items in our make-up, such as hair color, eye color, hemophilia (being a 'bleeder'), etc., are inherited through the agency of so-called dominant and recessive genes in a relatively straightforward and understandable way. However, there are many other characters—the "most fundamental and important characters of the organism" as stated by competent geneticists—which vary in *quantity* and in which many sets of genes are concerned. The "unknowns" referred to above are probably very important here and these characters cannot be predicted or accounted for by genetic calculations. Among these characters are form and development of various parts, fertility, intelligence, speed and strength.

As discussed in an earlier chapter, we have found in our laboratory that young rats appear to have inborn tendencies toward the consumption of more (or less) butter, sugar, salt, yeast, meat, alcohol, etc., and widely differing tendencies to exercise so that some may run two hundred feet a day and others six miles per day. *How* such tendencies as these are inherited is unknown, but they must be inherited, since the animals had all been kept in essentially the same environment prior to testing. These tendencies differ greatly even among animals that are the result of close inbreeding and hence should have in their make-up about the same assortment of genes. That the "unknowns" which govern differentiation are involved is highly probable. If this is so, it would make possible even in closely inbred animals the development, *by modified differentiation,* of endocrine glands and other organs of different sizes and activities.

We should not by any means limit our thinking about heredity to those items for which we have a clear-cut picture of the inheritance mechanism. If we do, we will be leaving out ninety-five per cent or more of the inheritance that must take place. Left out will be the "most fundamental and important characters" of all.

When an original fertilized egg cell that is to become a human being first divides into two cells, there are biological mechanisms which insure that the chromosomes and genes in the cell nucleus will be the same in the two "daughter" cells. There is no mechanism which insures that the rest of the complex structures within the original egg cell will be equally partitioned between the two daughter cells. Indeed, the internal structure of the original cell is so complicated and unsymmetrical that it is impossible for it to be divided to produce two daughter cells that are precisely the same in every particular. One cannot imagine cutting in two an irregularly shaped rock so that each half will be just like the other.

This is an important point because so-called "identical twins" (one-egg twins is a better designation) are produced when these two daughter cells develop separately into two individuals. It has often been assumed that one-egg twins have identical inheritance. This is true only with respect to the genes and chromosomes and not with respect to other cellular features which may also play an important role in inheritance.

Fraternal (two-egg) twins are produced when two separate eggs are fertilized by different spermatozoa at about the same time. There is nothing to insure that even the genes and chromosomes are identical, any more than there would be in the case of two children born at different times from the same father and mother. The inheritance of one-egg twins is therefore more alike (due to the chromosomes and genes being the same) than that of fraternal twins, but the inheritance of each of a pair of one-egg twins cannot be assumed to be completely identical because of the probable presence in the cellular material outside the genes and chromosomes of crucially important factors which are involved in the control of differentiation.

Many experiments have been performed by psychologists and by biologists, based on the assumption that one-egg twins have identical inheritance, and that if the two differ in any way, including intelligence, this difference must have been brought about by environmental influences. While one-egg twins are often remarkably alike in appearance, mentality and temperament, this likeness is far from uniform, and taking into account up-to-date knowledge, one cannot be at all sure that environmental influences are responsible for the differences that exist. The two cells from which they started were not identical in every particular. Sometimes the cells are very nearly alike and sometimes they have greater differences.

Inheritance in human beings and in all mammals is *exceedingly* complicated, as all competent geneticists know. Our findings and interpretations make it appear even more so. While the general principle of "like begets like" holds to a degree, the birth to humble parents of extraordinary individuals—like Lincoln—presents no special mystery in view of the extreme complexity of inheritance and our inability to predict with respect to the "most fundamental and important characters." Children are often remarkably different from their parents.

This is one reason why eugenics is so problematical. If we knew just how the most fundamental and important characters are inherited and could ascribe everything to simple gene action, we would be able to improve the race (or at least implement certain ideas about its improvement) by selective breeding. Of course, something can be done on the basis of what we now know and there are institutes which advise young people regarding marriage when they carry known genetic defects. But there is no way of assuring John and Mary, who carry no known genetic defects, what their progeny will be like. When they marry they gamble; the product of their union is bound to be unique and hopefully "normal" in the popular sense of the term.

The future of psychology holds many interesting innovations. There are many general phenomena which will still require extensive study and investigation—many of these could be considered as in the domain of sensory physiology—but it is in the vast realm involving the useful application of psychology to real individuals—not George Rutherford Adams—that the change will be greatest.

It was once supposed that people could be classified simply into two groups: *normal* and *abnormal*. While courses in "abnormal psychology" are still given in universities, this designation is no longer regarded as a good one. A prominent psychiatrist told me recently that he had made a careful and detailed study of a series of healthy people, but that he did not find among these a single one who was completely free from all the psychological symptoms that are sometimes associated with mental disease.

The problem of how to sort and classify people in a valid manner is a pressing one in connection with many activities. We need to be able to sort children so that they can be effectively educated—each to suit his or her own make-up. Children do not have exactly the same food requirements because of their biochemical individuality; we need to know how to sort them so they can all get what they need. The recreations that suit some individuals will not suit others at all. People need help in sorting themselves. We need to know how to sort people because of the fact that they will not need the same books, the same music or the same religion. Expertness must be developed in sorting people in connection with the selection of marriage mates, and in the field of medicine and psychiatry we need to learn how to sort people because they are by no means prone to have the same diseases. Expertness in sorting people is a challenging objective which must be sought in the decades to come. It will not be easy, but I have confidence that human minds, aided by computers, will find ways of accomplishing it.

Sorting in the past has been too much on a hit or miss, trial and error basis. While I would emphasize the right of every individual to live his own life and make his own choices—within reasonable limits—there is a vast deal that psychology and psychiatry can do, often in cooperation with the biological sciences, to make sensible choices easier.

It would not be seemly or wise for me to outline or discuss psychological sorting and classification as it may take place in the future. It would be too much like attempting to write a textbook on psychology. It does seem safe to say that the simple ratings—good–bad, normal–abnormal, intelligent–dumb, gifted–ungifted, exceptional–ordinary—are relatively worthless and may even be vicious. People are too complicated to be dealt with in this way.

Closely related to the problem of classification and sorting is an important objective in psychology and psychiatry, namely, the *prevention* of human disasters. We should not center all our attention on how to treat criminals, how to deal with broken homes, how to help the mentally retarded, how to aid those who are alcoholics or how to medicate the mentally ill. We need to *prevent* crime, *prevent* unhappy marriages and broken homes, *prevent* mental retardation, *prevent* alcoholism and drug addiction and *prevent* mental illness.

One very hopeful aspect is the fact that the mere recognition of inborn individuality by the public generally will help prevent many individuals from suffering the disaster incident to the psychological stress of trying to live a lie. Such recognition would eliminate the trauma which results from trying to force children and adults into preconceived and inappropriate molds.

The prevention of mental retardation is an eminently worthy cause and it hurts me to know that in years past it has received so little attention in comparison with the immediate problem of dealing with the mentally retarded children we have already produced. There is good reason to think that whenever a child's mind doesn't work right, this is attributable to some metabolic weakness or defect in the thinking apparatus—the brain. If the parents have adequate mentalities, one place to look for the source of the trouble is in the prenatal nutrition of the infant. That this is a very likely place to look is emphasized by the fact that in experimental animals in the laboratory we can regularly cause healthy parents to produce defective young of all descriptions, merely by giving the prospective mother a deficient diet during the period of gestation. In some cases a vitamin, for example, needs to be missing for only a short time during gestation to produce malformed young, provided the lack comes at a critical time in the life of the fetus.

When we realize that nutrition is to a degree an individual matter and that all mothers and all fetuses do not have precisely the same food requirements, this magnifies the probability that mental retardation may have prenatal malnutrition as its basis. The first practical approach is to get everybody, including physicians, the public and prospective mothers, to become more nutrition-conscious and more aware of what is already known. After this we need to know more about individual needs—how to spot them and how to sort people with respect to their biochemical individuality.

Psychologists need to be aware of the nutritional and biochemical aspects of diseases involving the mind. In recent years it has been discovered that a metabolic defect—too much production of phenyl pyruvic acid and its accumulation in the blood—causes brain damage accompanied by mental retardation and even idiocy, if not treated. When an infant having this metabolic defect is fed a diet almost devoid of phenyl alanine (one of the essential amino acids) for a time, the production of phenyl pyruvic acid decreases and the damage is halted. Later the child may be able to eat ordinary food, and proceed without further difficulty. This is only one of several causes of mental retardation and it does not involve large numbers. In other rare cases babies tend to accumulate galactose in the blood; this causes brain damage and mental deficiency. If milk sugar (lactose) is eliminated from their diet, the damaging effects of galactose are eliminated. These ameliorative measures are excellent when they work. They point to the probability that all mental deficiencies have a biochemical basis and that many of them can be prevented by special care with respect to prenatal nutrition.

We have already had something to say in previous chapters about the prevention of crime and of alcoholism. The prevention of mental disease is certainly an important objective for psychiatrists and clinical psychologists. Students in this area have become increasingly aware of the importance of biochemical individuality as it affects drug action (page 134) and of the fact that susceptibility to mental disease varies greatly from individual to individual. Some people go through life suffering all kinds of frustrations and trouble without mental disease; others succumb with comparatively little provocation. This is a difficult field in which to work, but again I believe that human minds will find a way to prevent mental disease even in those who are prone toward this kind of trouble. Prenatal and postnatal malnutrition should receive continuous attention as a possible source of difficulty.

CHAPTER XII

What
of
Philosophy?

An elementary conclusion we can draw from considering a world where every mind is innately highly distinctive is that *not everyone will care for philosophy*. I notice this is in my own family of four brothers, all of whom graduated from college and were exposed to the subject. One of us couldn't like anything better; it is definitely his dish. Another brother couldn't care for it any less. The other two—which includes me—are between the two extremes in this regard; we have had some interest in quite different aspects but in unconventional ways.

It is no news to professors of philosophy that some students are uninterested in philosophical study, but a lack of such interest may be interpreted to mean lack of a "good" mind or of a favorable upbringing. Variable interest in philosophy is often due, however, to innate variability in people's mental patterns. It would be most unfortunate if every person's mind turned strongly toward philosophical contemplations; there are so many nonphilosophical jobs that need to be done.

This is not to disparage philosophy; it is a subject that should be studied generally in every university. Everyone has a philosophy which he lives by, whether he recognizes it as such or not. This is true of housewives, bankers, politicians, priests, rabbis and preachers, truck drivers—everybody. Oftentimes the real philosophy by which an individual lives may be quite at variance with what he would profess openly. I heard a scientist spoken of in an uncomplimentary way as following the philosophy of a dog—purported to be: "If he finds anything he can't eat or copulate with, he urinates on it." This doesn't, I am sure, do justice either to a dog or to the man with whom the dog was compared.

If we recognize the inborn individuality of men's minds, we will draw a second conclusion: *every philosopher will disagree with every other philosopher*. Possibly we should put it positively: agreement between philosophers, when it exists, will be only *in spots*. How would it sound to say, "Professor Aloysius Alphonsus [I made up this name!] is a great philosopher—the greatest in this century; his ideas are in complete agreement with those of David Hume"? Unless a philosopher contributes something in the way of disagreement, he is no philosopher.

Philosophers of different ages have vastly different assortments of knowledge, information and ideas on which to build, but even if they built on the same foundation, they would not build alike.

In a book on twentieth-century philosophers by Morton White, chairman of the Philosophy Department at Harvard, I found evidence in the very first paragraph of an apparent lack of appreciation of the diversity of men's minds and an apparent search for a philosophy that would be "the real McCoy." White said in effect that almost every important philosophical movement of the twentieth century started out by finding fault with Hegel, who was "enormously muddled." This leads one to ask: Who decides who is muddled and who isn't? How many minor muddlers would it take to unmuddle one big muddler? I am not defending Hegel (except in his right to be muddled) nor am I suggesting that no progress is possible in the field of philosophy. What I am trying to suggest, perhaps in a naïve and inexpert way, is that variety is the spice of philosophy as well as of life. No one can hope to find the one thoroughly unmuddled philosophy on which everyone will agree. Because of the inborn individuality of our minds this would be as impossible as to find a diet (or a cheese) that just suits everybody or a drug that will have precisely the same effect on everyone who takes it.

What is important in a philosophy can be decided only on the basis of its utility (in the broadest sense) and its wide acceptance as useful and beneficent by succeeding generations of people. The best philosopher, as well as I can see, is the one who makes his ideas click most constructively; they continue to click century after century in the minds of many people.

If people's minds were not distinctive and different from one another, books on philosophy would not have been written, and as a subject for study, philosophy wouldn't exist. If we were all under the control of our environments, we would all fall into the same general patterns of thinking and there would be nothing of consequence to write about in a philosophical way. Socrates, Plato and Aristotle would not have been heard of if their minds had been just like those of their contemporaries. If all philosophers had like minds, philosophy would be dead.

While passing judgments on philosophers is not a pastime I would choose, I have strong suspicions that many philosophers have fallen into the same man-trap of overgeneralization that Stuart Chase describes. They have probably suffered from "universalitis"; have not been content to limit themselves to what they might reasonably know about *men,* but have preferred grandiose erudite discussions about "man." Many times philosophical writing could be improved if the writers would ask themselves two questions: "How could I know that?" and "What of it?"

My thinking about overgeneralizations (which I encounter often) has made me supersensitive. For example, if one writes a book or article having to do with *"the* child" (this has been done many times), this is an effective way of overgeneralizing without calling attention to the fact that a generalization has been made. It *implies* (but is careful not to state) that all children are alike and that the prototype, *child,* should be our primary concern. Similarly, one may surreptitiously generalize about *the* newspaper reader, *the* churchgoer or *the* criminal. The honest thing is to speak of "children," "newspaper readers," "churchgoers," "criminals." If one wants to make generalizations, he can then do so at his own risk; the sneaky thing to do is to try to get the generalization by without stating it.

This same kind of generalization has even been bootlegged into the scientific field by the expressions: *"the* cell" (implying that all cells are the same); *"the* cell wall" (implying that all cells have the same walls); *"the* rat" (implying that all rats are the same); *"the* chemical bond" (implying that they are all the same); *"the* atom" (as though they were all the same). It would be fairer and far safer to talk about "cells," "cell walls," "rats," "chemical bonds" and "atoms" and then bring out *into the open,* after careful scrutiny, whatever generalizations may be justified.

In talking to myself about this kind of implied overgeneralization, I have called it "*the* thinking," though actually it does not necessarily involve the use of the word "*the*." "Man" is another way of saying "*the* human being," and "protoplasm" is another way of saying "*the* living substance." I remember over thirty-five years ago objecting to the word protoplasm. Fortunately, it is being used less and less. Its complete abandonment is appropriate now that electron microscope pictures show it not to be a gooey "substance" but instead full of structural features.

Interestingly, this bad habit of "*the* thinking" has not invaded all fields. I have never heard of an astronomy lecture on *the* star, *the* heavenly body or *the* galaxy. I have never heard of mathematicians holding forth learnedly on *the* number, *the* statistic or *the* algebraic symbol. I have never heard of an erudite literary lecture on *the* modern book.

I even dislike the expression "*the* individual" on similar grounds. I have never been able to understand just what it means. Is it all individuals rolled into one and divided by the total number? If so, it has no individuality. "*The* individual" carries (to me) an internal contradiction; if it is a prototype, it is a hypothetical average and not an *individual* at all. If you do not keep step with me in these thoughts and observations, it must be that your mind does not work just like mine. In the words of Thoreau, you hear "a different drummer."

One of the axioms or self-evident truths that some people carry in their minds continuously is something like this: "Life must be simple in its essence" or "If we understood life, everything would fall into place nicely." While I certainly endorse the idea of trying to set down our thoughts in understandable words, anyone who accepts these axioms might be hard put to swallow and digest the facts of human individuality. On the other hand, failure to accept these facts places one in a worse dilemma—that of facing a world of the future when human perplexity and thought are no longer necessary.

According to the best available knowledge, human beings have been on this earth hundreds of thousands of years and there is no reason to believe that they will not be here for hundreds of thousands of years to come. Even if we attempt to blow ourselves up, we will fail and plenty of specimens will be left. If inborn individuality did not exist to a high degree—all our concern would in this case be concentrated on developing a uniform, favorable environment—basic human problems could be shortly solved. Then what? It seems fair that we think of our neighbors far and near both in time as well as space. What a hell this world would be for people (our progeny) with expanding minds if there was nothing left to be puzzled about!

The Divine Plan has taken care of all this; human individuality does exist and plenty of practical problems will confront the members of the human race a thousand years from now. The facts of human individuality give us a guarantee that life will never be reduced to formulas; it will never be simple, cut and dried and completely uninteresting.

The progress of science is in line with this concept. Has science worked in the direction of "buttoning up" one problem after another? Can we say that we are half the way through or one fifth the way or one tenth the way? Not by any means. Whenever we carefully ask nature a question, we get some kind of answer but it is often a qualified one; and if we are alert, we find an expanding number of new questions which we have an urge to answer. It has often been said that science raises more questions than it answers. This is why science can go on and on without exhausting itself. A scientist of fifty years ago could not possibly envisage what the present holds; a scientist of today cannot envisage what will come fifty years hence. Furthermore, there are, because of human individuality, plenty of intriguing problems still *on earth*. We do not need to go to outer space to find them. On the other hand, there is no one to prevent us from taking space trips if we can afford to pay the fare, and to spend the time.

The acceptance of the facts of human individuality has a humbling as well as an ennobling effect on our attitudes. Although scientists should do the utmost with their minds, they should recognize limitations; they should not expect that they will be able to understand the universe and everything that is in it. A man should not "think of himself more highly than he ought to think." Einstein, who had less reason to feel modest than most of us, said, "Before God we are all equally wise, equally foolish."

We should not expect too much of our philosophy; we are gods but we should not forget that we are *little* gods. A newspaper editor of three generations ago said, "In this great universe of ours man is a mere insect, an ant in his intellect —as measured by the intelligence capable of grasping the whole of truth and knowledge." This was written many years ago before the day of modern physics and astronomy, when compared to modern concepts, the universe was conceived to be about peanut-size. If man appeared like an insect then, he would appear now as an ultramicroscopic fleck of animated dust. We can take great pride in the fact that we have discovered our own smallness and that our limitations may not be as severe as they superficially appear to be. We should continue to do the utmost with our minds (and everything that this term may encompass) but we should be mature enough to see our intellects in some reasonable perspective and not expect them to encompass everything. This is using common sense.

One of the philosophical lines of thought which is related to that of the origin of life, the origin of thinking and the origin of moral responsibility—discussed in an earlier chapter—has to do with chance and probabilities. My interest in this has been stimulated by the statement, made more or less in jest, that if you gave a bunch of monkeys typewriters and let them peck away *long enough,* they would write all the books in the British Museum.

For amusement when I was on an airplane trip I thought it would be diverting to calculate how long it would take a monkey working at random to write something simple that would make sense. I chose the sentence: *Man is the result of monkey business.* This would require thirty-eight consecutive correct pecks on a typewriter (including the shift key for the capital M). Since there are about ninety different marks (or spaces) to be registered with a typewriter, the chances are one in ninety that the first punch would be the right one; the chances that the first two punches will be the right two is one in 90^2; the chances that the first three punches will be the correct one is one in 90^3 (729,000), etc.

If we assume for simplicity and to speed things up, that the monkey will (1) peck away in a random fashion (not concentrating, for example, on the space bar or repeating the same letter over and over); (2) use the typewriter and the shift key properly and not jam the machine; (3) that there is an "overseer" who will let the monkey make thirty-eight jabs and then instantaneously shift the carriage back and put in a fresh slip of paper; (4) that the monkey is a speedster and a scab and completes thirty-eight pecks each ten seconds of a twenty-four-hour day, without a coffee or coconut milk break—under these favorable circumstances, how long before he may be expected to write the correct sentence?

The answer, even in terms of billions of years, would reach completely across a page and would require nineteen commas to set it off.*

Since our earth is only a few billion years old, writing a simple sentence in this way would be preposterously hopeless for one monkey or even for a billion monkeys with a billion typewriters and a billion "overseers." The amount of paper used up in this little (?) experiment would weigh millions of times as much as our entire solar system! Obviously, this is one of the poorest ways imaginable to write a book.

I found, subsequent to my simple calculation, that the late Norbert Wiener, famous M.I.T. mathematician, had disposed of the monkey-typewriter idea in quite a different way. He indicated that even if the monkeys had completed all possible books of 1,000,000 words or less (some *if!*), the library would be such an uncatalogued mess that it would be completely useless. It would take a Shakespeare to pick *Hamlet* out of the huge mess; as much genius would be required to find it and select it as to write it.

The theory of probability tells what is probable when a series of trials is made, but it gives us no assurance as to the exact course of events. We cannot count on the sentence's being correctly written by a monkey in 90^{38} trials nor that it

* The chance that the first 38 pecks will yield the correct sentence is one in 90^{38}. To make the chances one in one, 38 pecks must be repeated 90^{38} times. This would take 10×90^{38} seconds. There are 31,536,000 seconds in a year, so the time reduced to years would be approximately 20×90^{34} years. Reduced to thousands of years it would be about 160×90^{28}, and to billions of years, about 90^{26}. This 90^{26} is a huge number requiring 59 digits.

will take that many trials to do the job. The correct sentence might come up for a given monkey on the first day, without conflicting with probability theory. *On the average,* however, if the correct sentence is written many times (think how long this would take!), it will take 90^{38} trials to do the job.

If a deck of cards is dealt for bridge, it is extremely unlikely that one of the players will get thirteen cards of one suit, yet this and other most unusual things can happen and they may happen much earlier than might be expected on the basis of probability theory. I have played poker very few times in my life—possibly fifty or a hundred hands in all—and yet on one occasion I was *dealt* a royal flush—a very improbable event. If the cards have the right arrangement, what seems most improbable will certainly happen.

The same principle may apply to the question of how life, thinking and conscience came to originate on this earth. Perhaps the cards of the universe—presumably all the laws under which it operates—are arranged so that these developments were bound to occur. I would assume that the laws are stable and do not shift; in other words, we need not concern ourselves with many different sets of laws—only one set. What may seem most improbable, thinking in terms of shuffled sets of laws, may happen at once with a particular set that has been prearranged.

We may not be able to think of all the prearrangements necessary to make life, thinking and conscience possible; possibly our progeny a few generations later, through gaining a more comprehensive knowledge of the laws of nature, will have a better idea. It seems reasonably satisfying at present to conclude that the marvelous developments on this earth came about because a suitably prearranged deck—involving a multitude of coordinated natural laws—was the starting point.

We do not know the ground rules—the complete laws

and the nature of life—well enough to calculate how long it might take life to originate under the conditions that prevailed when it happened.

It would appear that the origin and development of life bear little resemblance to the writing of a book by a monkey. There hasn't been time—not by a factor of trillions of trillions of trillions—for a monkey to write even a simple sentence.

CHAPTER XIII

The Utmost with Our Minds

Everything we do with our minds is related to the distinctive equipment we possess. We are born in the chains of ignorance and lack of comprehension; the first task our brains have to do from the beginning is to interpret the messages that come from the sense receptors all over the body. These messages would be unique for each of us even if our environments were identical, because our message-collecting and -sending equipment is also distinctive for each. These messages are the only raw material with which our brains can work.

Without interpretation these single "yes" signals coming by the millions from millions of sites would be as meaningless as the naked electrical impulses we get from a space vehicle photographing the moon. It is no wonder that for this tremendous task our brains are equipped with billions of nerve cells of various types. To a newborn baby these signals are mostly meaningless, but gradually over a period of years they take over more and more meaning and we make sense out of many of the signals that come to us. If our interpretative powers are limited we may never arrive, even by extensive training, at the point where the signals coming from a complex mathematical formula or from something written in a foreign tongue will be comprehended.

As we have noted, the numerous types of sense receptors (page 37) have not even been satisfactorily classified, and the kind of information the individual types are built to give are for the most part still unknown. Many of the receptors pertain to the traditional senses: seeing, hearing, touching, tasting and smelling, but there are many types of receptors completely outside the areas concerned with the traditional senses.

The sense of taste, according to tradition, merely allows us to know if some substance is sweet, sour, salty, bitter or tasteless, but the brain work accompanying tasting is far more complicated than this breakdown suggests. For example, *salty*, as descriptive of a taste, is not satisfying to one who has a chemical training. Ordinarily, *salty* means the response elicited by *sodium chloride*, but what about other salts: *potassium chloride, sodium iodide, rubidium chloride, potassium sulfate* or *ammonium acetate*, etc.? They may all taste salty if one uses the term to cover the sensations received from all of them, but they are distinguishable from each other; they do not all taste just alike. *Bitter* is not perfectly definite in its meaning. There are hundreds of chemicals that might be called *bitter*, but they do not necessarily elicit exactly the same sensation. No one can be sure that the bitter of quinine, hops, cascara and grapefruit are all the same. That our equipment in regard to interpreting tastes is distinctive is shown by the fact that people may register entirely different taste sensations from the same substance (page 125).

The sense of smell is even more complicated because there are literally thousands of chemicals which have somewhat distinctive odors, and the brain of one whose equipment is suitable and highly trained can distinguish many of these, presumably by interpreting various combinations of impulses. Of course, the equipment possessed by each of us is unique; some people are partially or wholly without sense of smell (anosmic), and individuals differ markedly both in what they can smell and what seems pleasant.

The sense of hearing also involves highly complicated brain work. There are vibrations through a wide range of frequency which we may be able to hear, distinguish and remember if our equipment is suitable. Pitch discrimination, possession of absolute pitch, ability to play "by ear," judging tonal intensity, hearing harmony with discrimination and appreciation, timing, being able to recognize individual voices, or to understand conversation in a noisy background—these all involve the extremely complex working of our brains, and the degrees to which we possess various types of abilities and can receive training in them is highly distinctive, as Carl E. Seashore has clearly shown in his *Psychology of Music*.

The sense of touch is also complicated and it requires little-understood brain work to decipher the messages. Deep pressure stimulates different nerve endings from those involved when the pressure is light. The sense of tickle which is possessed by some individuals to a high degree and is practically absent in others is not well understood but is related to the sense of touch. Some individuals experience a disagreeable cringe when, for example, the fuzz of a peach touches their skin, particularly their lips. Others feel no such sensation. Each of us has, near the surface of the skin, a distinctive set of nerve endings for cold, warm and pain, so that two spots a sixteenth of an inch apart may have distinctive characteristics (page 39). Messages from all these nerve endings must be interpreted by our brains.

The sense of sight illustrates well the extensive brain work which is involved in the common senses. We are quite mistaken if we suppose that we *see* something *first* and then use our brains to think about it. We can't see anything unless our brains function. Even the throwing of satisfactory images on the two retinas involves some brain work because of the necessity of opening and closing the diaphragms (iris) and focusing, but the production of good images is only the first step. Our brains must learn that the images are on the retina, grasp every detail of them in color from messages sent by the millions of individual nerve receptors, and interpret the images as meaning the presence, quite outside the eyes, of *one* object for each *two* images—not one for each retinal image. If our brains are poisoned with alcohol, for example, or the nervous setup is otherwise damaged, the two images may be interpreted as two objects (double vision). Our brains never make the mistake of locating the object where the image is. The house we see in the distance is seen *in the distance* and is not interpreted to be *in our eyes*.

Several years ago at the Dartmouth Eye Institute, I had the opportunity of witnessing, with the guidance of the late Dr. Adelbert Ames, a demonstration which showed clearly that what we *see* (even with one eye) is really a meaningful *interpretation* of the image which is on the retina. An image was thrown successively on the retina (also on the ground glass in a camera) which originated from three different external objects of different shapes and configurations. They were viewed, however, from such an angle that they all produced about the same image. One of the objects was meaningful—a common chair outlined in string. Another was a

highly distorted chairlike object. The third was a meaningless hodgepodge of strings so arranged in space, however,
that when viewed from the proper angle, they yielded virtually the same image as that produced by the chair made of
strings. When the images from these three external objects
are successively observed from an appropriate angle, no one
sees the distorted chair or the hodgepodge of strings. Everyone sees an upright chair, since this makes sense in the light
of past experience. We see *what makes the most sense, not
necessarily the external object.*

This particular demonstration was only one of several,
all pointing to the interpretative work involved when we
see. What we see is not necessarily what "meets the eye" but
rather what "meets the brain." When we have optical illusions our brains interpret incorrectly. In connection with
these interpretative operations there is color vision, depth
perception, speed perception, spatial imagery, estimation of
distances, estimation of angles, the sense of pleasing design,
and the sense of fusion which is involved in seeing moving
pictures—all these involving the functioning of the brain
equipment which can *interpret* in complex ways what is
happening on the retinas. Since our brain equipment as well
as our eyes is distinctive, each of us has a unique set of abilities—and the ability to receive training—in all these respects.

Among the senses, other than the traditional ones, with
which we are all equipped—unequally—is the sense of
equilibrium. The vestibular portions of our inner ears are
equipped with special devices, including nerve receptors,
which send messages that are interpreted by our brains in
terms of our balance, when as in walking, for example, we
continually throw ourselves forward and out of balance and
then catch ourselves with the next step. The mechanisms involved can be trained, but as usual they vary in the amount

of training they can receive. As people age, these mechanisms play out—the nerve endings may actually die off gradually—and as a result an aged person tends to be unsteady on his feet and more liable to fall.

Related to this equilibrium sense is the "position" or kinesthetic sense which is associated with the flow of messages from special sense receptors, possibly the Pacinian corpuscles (page 37). These make it possible for us to know without the use of other senses, when we are fully awake, how our arms and legs, for example, are positioned. This sense may remain asleep after we awaken and gain consciousness, in which case we may be quietly in bed for a short time without having any knowledge of the position we are lying in or where our arms and legs are placed. These nerve endings start functioning soon, however, and send messages from their positions in muscles, joints and tendons, giving our brain the raw material from which it derives the kind of information we usually take for granted.

It may safely be presumed that all of the various types of nerve endings which exist pick up sensations and send messages to the brain. As long as there remains any ignorance as to how many kinds of nerve endings there are, or what each one does (it will take many years to catch up on all this), there is room for the discovery of new and hitherto unrecognized senses, or of new aspects of the senses that are already recognized. Recently I have read reports of people being able to detect and differentiate between certain colors through contact with the skin. We are not in a position to say categorically that this is impossible until we know about the workings of every kind of nerve ending.

One sense about which we know little is the sense of direction. Some people are easily "turned around" as we say. If they go into a building and pass through a few hallways or turn a few street corners, the only directions they can be sure about are *up* and *down*. Others retain their sense of direction well even in more complicated situations. That the sense of direction in dogs, cats and birds (homing pigeons, for example) is often keen is well known. It would appear that they may carry with them physiological registering compasses which make it possible for them to "remember" automatically every turn their bodies take. Because of these automatic registering compasses, their directions are never confused.

Another sense about which we know relatively little is "time sense," involving primarily the ability to estimate time. We vary greatly from one another in our time sense, and when one becomes mentally ill or even if one has a fever, the time-estimating mechanism, whatever it is, may be badly thrown off. But it recovers when health is restored.

It should not be imagined that this time sense is vague or questionable. Its presence is observed throughout the biological kingdom. Even insects carry tiny biological clocks (watches?) around with them. It has been found that cockroaches kept in cages where their running activities can be recorded will become active at twenty-four-hour intervals, timed practically to the minute. This happens when they have access to the effects of daylight and dark. If they are kept continually in total darkness, they do not lose their sense of time but their watches run faster and individual watches then show differences. Under these conditions one cockroach, for example, followed his activity pattern every twenty-two hours and ten minutes; another every twenty-three hours and eighteen minutes, with errors of not more than two minutes per day. When these cockroaches were returned to where they could see daylight and dark, they reverted to the precise twenty-four-hour schedule. The fact that the time sense in cockroaches and in many other forms of life must have a physiological (anatomical) basis suggests that in human beings also there are physiological mechanisms involved. We know nothing, however, about these.

Our brains are also equipped—unequally—with respect to interpretative operations which seem to be quite beyond those of ordinary sensory reception. We all of us are capable, for example, of developing some *mathematical sense.* We may be—like William Lyon Phelps—"slow but not sure," or we may take to it readily. This sense gives us the conviction that two plus two is really four and that $(a+b)^2 = a^2 + 2ab + b^2$, regardless of whether the teacher says so or not. When Einstein as a small youngster began to play with algebra and geometry, he used his eyes, for example, to see what he read and wrote, but what he *saw* (his interpretation of the nerve impulses that came to his brain from his retinas) was a great deal more than most children of his age would have "seen." His innate mathematical sense was keen and easily cultivated. It is obvious that the mathematical sense of different individuals is not the same, and in some cases the sense is not to be trusted.

We all have, to varying degrees, a *sense of logic.* Take the proposition: if A is B, and B is C, then A is C. It takes the working of our minds to tell whether or not this is so. If one has to accept or reject such propositions on the basis of "what the authorities say," he is lacking in logical sense. Our brains are equipped to make such interpretations and draw appropriate conclusions.

We are all equipped, to varying degrees, with what we may call *language sense.* This is a broad category. When two babies hear language spoken, they grasp—unequally—what it is all about. Some talk very early, showing that their language sense is easily cultivated and that they hear and interpret readily. This precocity does not mean that mathematical sense is also possessed in high degree; the two senses seem to be largely independent. The possession of mathematical sense in high degree does not tell anything about one's language sense. Einstein was very slow in learning to talk, so much so that his parents were concerned about him. Even at nine years of age he was halting and slow in his speech. The ways in which people develop language sense are not the same. Some can learn language if they hear it spoken; others can learn it readily (that is, learn to read) from books. In any case, the brain work involved is unmistakable.

The important role played by the brain in such instances can hardly be exaggerated. This is illustrated by the case of Helen Keller, who was effectively shackled, it might seem, by blindness and deafness. She had to receive most of her messages from the outside world from her teacher through the medium of touch (pressure), but if she had possessed a less keen mind she would not have been able to make sense of the world around her even with her patient teacher's help. Her interpretative brain work was marvelous. That she had a brilliant and receptive mind is clear both from her precocity as an infant, before she lost her sight and hearing, and her high academic record and her subsequent literary and other activities—even in the absence of sight and hearing.

What is the exact province of *science* and what kind of mental equipment do scientists use in their work? In a current biology book which is before me I read that by self-imposed limitations science "deals only with material things"— "things that can be seen, heard, felt, tasted and smelt, with no others." This view, which is widely held, sounds like a plausible one, but when one considers it in the light of our discussion, many questions raise their heads.

Can we *see*, excluding all *interpretations?* Can we accept only what we *hear* and reject all the interpretations that our brains furnish? Can we separate what we feel, taste and smell from the interpretations which our brains furnish when messages come from the nerve receptors? Mathematics cannot be seen, heard, felt, tasted or smelled; is it automatically banished from the field of science? Logic is not to be seen, heard, felt, tasted or smelled; is it an outcast so far as science is concerned? Are the sense of equilibrium, the sense of direction, the sense of timing excluded from science and is the door closed forever to the discovery of new senses?

All of these questions can be answered with an emphatic *"No."* I come back to the quotation from Percy Bridgeman: "The vital feature of the scientist's procedure has been to do the utmost with his mind, no holds barred." If scientists exclude all the interpretative functions of the brain, including the mathematical sense and the sense of logic, they have nothing left to work with.

The thinking of scientists should not be strait-jacketed; they should be allowed and encouraged to tackle any subject that they hope to shed light on, and they may need to use all the senses and all the sense they have, no holds barred. There are, of course, some subjects that seem more suitable than others for scientific study, and there are some senses that are more dependable than others and will be used more often. Unless a sense is widely possessed with some degree of uniformity, it is relatively useless in science. The senses of smell, taste and feeling, for example, are rarely used in any critical way in the fields of chemistry or physics for the reason that they vary greatly from one individual to another and hence are not dependable.

There are a number of other "senses" associated with the functioning of the brain which are of highest significance and importance. Many of these are possessed very unequally by real people; some are more "dependable" than others.

Intuitive sense, like language sense, covers much territory. When we have intuition, we unconsciously gather together and integrate everything that we know or have observed that has any bearing on a subject, and on this basis (which may be broad or not so broad) we have a hunch that such and such will happen or will prove to be true. The use of intuitive sense is in principle just like seeing. When we *see*, we accept the meaningless impulses, and using our memories of what has gone before, we make sense out of them. When we have an intuition, we take many memories of past interpretations and make sense out of them.

Like "seeing" or "mathematical sense," intuition is not always to be trusted. There are many optical illusions in which we think we see what we don't see, but in general we find it wise to trust our eyesight. There have been many mathematical ideas presented which are not regarded as sound, yet we find that mathematical sense is on the whole trustworthy.

The reliability of intuition cannot be regarded as highly as that of seeing, but it is nonetheless widely used by scientists and others. Our own intuitions we tend to take seriously; the intuitions of others, unless they coincide with ours, we tend to discount. Seeing is believing, but what the other fellow sees doesn't carry the same conviction second-hand.

Without intuition a scientist wouldn't know what to do —which of the innumerable possible experiments to attempt (no one could think of doing them all). In order to select one which promises to yield interesting answers the scientist unconsciously gathers together everything pertinent that he knows and evolves a hunch. If he is widely experienced in the area and if he has good intuitive faculties, his hunch is much more likely to be sound than if his knowledge is limited. The importance of the "good intuitive faculties" is hard to exaggerate, however, because outstanding discoveries have resulted from the application of these faculties by those who are naïve and not afraid to stick out their necks.

Intuition has played an enormous role in the contributions of such great scientists as Pasteur, Newton and Darwin; anyone who is a searcher after truth must use it. Einstein has said, "Imagination is more important than knowledge." Albert Szent-Gyorgyi, a Nobel Prize winner, has said, "Research is not a systematic occupation; it is an intuitive, artistic vocation—in spite of all the hard work involved." Of course, all scientists recognize that intuitions should be put to the acid test of experiment whenever this is possible.

The tremendous role of intuition in human life is emphasized when we consider that while scientific interpretations have a way of getting out of date—sometimes very rapidly—intuition with respect to matters that cannot be subjected to direct experiment may endure for centuries. Isaiah, Confucius and Gautama Buddha were approximately contemporaries about twenty-five hundred years ago. Each of these men, by intuition (or inspiration if you wish), expressed ideas that are as valid and up-to-date as if they had been uttered yesterday.

In our own day intuition is of tremendous value in the fields of business and human relations. Some men have an almost uncanny ability to judge others and to pick "winners." Some know intuitively what is likely to happen. If it is something bad they may say, "I smell a rat." Of course, they don't literally smell anything, but the messages from the outside world which come to them by way of the nerve receptors are interpreted as being similar to a bad odor.

The value of intuitions depends on whose intuitions they are. If it were possible in science, business, politics or religion to select those with the highest intuitive powers, this would mark a big advance. A nationally prominent businessman with many diverse successes to his credit, told me, "When you are fifty-five per cent sure, it is time to act. If you wait until you are ninety-five per cent sure, the show is all over."

Many of the senses which we have the brain equipment to develop are of less importance in the field of science and more important elsewhere. One of the outstanding of these is the sense of beauty. While there is beauty in science and in mathematics, it does not play as large a role as in music, literature, poetry, sculpture, drama, painting. It would be most difficult to tell anyone who doesn't have a sense of beauty what beauty is. If one has this sense, he doesn't need to be told. People differ greatly in their ability to appreciate beauty in different areas. Those who are not equipped to understand the niceties of chemistry could find no beauty in it, and those relatively few who have no ear for music cannot appreciate its beauty. Probably everyone has a sense of beauty at least in some areas.

Appreciation of beauty involves the possession of suitable equipment; it is a contribution *we make individually,* using our own minds. A sunset may offer all kinds of intricate vibration patterns which are registered on our retinas, but unless our brains contribute by way of interpretation, it cannot be beautiful. Unless it is beautiful *to me,* its potential value is lost—to me.

The universality of the love of beauty in its various forms is a striking fact. While people are individually spotted in their ability to appreciate particular kinds of beauty and their individual tastes differ, the sense of beauty —the idea that some things are beautiful and elevating and others are ugly and disagreeable—is widespread among all the peoples of the world.

Musical sense or the appreciation of beauty in music depends upon the sense of hearing, but it is quite probable that a person could have good hearing, excellent pitch discrimination and much of the equipment necessary for hearing music and yet not be greatly impressed by its beauty. Brain equipment is crucial. An infant may listen to music; the nerve receptors are in working order but the ability to interpret is limited. The readiness with which children interpret music and the depth of their interpretation vary greatly from one child to another. To cite an extreme example, Mozart had the equipment to hear and interpret music very early. He played the harpsichord at three, composed when he was four, and played before the emperor at the age of six. It wasn't necessary to explain to him about music's being beautiful.

Musical sense is so widespread that in spite of the fact that some have relatively little of it, music is to a remarkable degree a universal language. Even during a cold war Van Cliburn was appreciated and acclaimed in Moscow.

Literary sense involves the appreciation of beauty in literature. If one doesn't have it, no amount of explaining will give it to him. Students who have little literary sense cannot be bludgeoned into loving literature dearly. A person who has literary sense doesn't need to go to college to find out what literature is. All he needs is access to books; the love takes hold in no uncertain way.

Poetic sense is a variant of literary sense. Matthew Arnold said of poetry, "It is the most beautiful, impressive and widely effective way of saying things." Literal-minded people have fathered the unfortunate expression "more truth than poetry," as though truth and poetry were in opposing camps. Poetry is a beautiful way—often using figurative language—of *telling the truth.*

Sense of humor involves a distinctive kind of interpretation by our brains; it is widely but very unequally possessed by members of the human family. Just as some people can in the physical sense be tickled easily and others effectively resist efforts in this direction, there are those who, like Mark Twain, are susceptible to being tickled mentally (and are capable of tickling others) and others to whom funny stories simply *are not funny,* because of a lack of equipment to interpret them that way. Probably something can be done to cultivate people's sense of humor—this would be desirable —but it would be very difficult to explain funniness to someone who has never experienced anything that struck him funny.

"Card sense" is not of first-order magnitude in importance, but in the field of recreation it is important and very unequally possessed by different people—quite independent of their other mental equipment. A brilliant mathematician can have it, but he can be almost lacking in it. It is not completely general; an individual may have the equipment to play one card game well but be incapable of excelling in another. Different card games involve different facets of our distinctive mental equipment.

Social sense is something that our own minds and natures contribute to the interpretation of the world around us. We do not have to be told that other people are important. One of the important ingredients of good social sense is the ability to remember people—also their names. Much can be developed in this area, yet social sense comes easily to some and is difficult to cultivate in others. The basic need of individuals for each other is probably universal.

Moral sense is not far removed from some of the other "senses" we have been discussing. The nerve impulses we get from the outside world are meaningless until our brains interpret their meaning. They have no moral implications whatever until our minds, gathering together everything we know and have learned, contribute to the interpretation "This is right" or "This is wrong."

While we are influenced in our judgments as to exactly what is right or what is wrong by the culture in which we live, we ourselves contribute the conviction that there is a difference between right and wrong, regardless of just where we draw the line. The dependence for many people's ideas of what is right and what is wrong and cultural environment on custom can be overemphasized. Francis of Assisi's ideas of right and wrong were not dictated by his cultural environment; neither were those of Martin Luther. This does not deny that many people have sheeplike tendencies in these regards.

It would be difficult to explain what conscience is to one who has never felt the prick of conscience. Try explaining to a horse the beauties of poetry and music and see how it goes! Fortunately, the moral sense doesn't need explaining to most people. They have it; it often arises very early in life and from the working of their own minds. In some it is comparatively keen; in some it becomes smothered. It is the function of churches, synagogues and other religious organizations to keep this sense from being smothered. They cannot create a moral sense where it does not already exist. The sense of love and devotion is something that *we* contribute to the interpretation of the world around us. If there is anyone who has never experienced true love and devotion—this can be quite apart from sex—he or she can hardly be told what love is or persuaded that it is good. Fortunately, the essence of love and devotion is spread widely throughout the world. It needs to be fostered.

It is interesting that Helen Keller, without sight or hearing, developed a keen sense of beauty, a literary sense and a profound moral sense of love and devotion. These came out of her own brain work. She didn't depend on her teacher to explain what was beautiful or what was right or wrong. This was part of her own remarkable development.

As a scientist whose primary interest is in *human biochemistry,* how many of the senses mentioned above, and others not mentioned, will I take cognizance of? How many will I use as tools?

I will certainly adopt the policy of doing the utmost with my mind, no holds barred, and will therefore feel free to use every sense that I find useful—certainly any of the traditional senses, as well as mathematical sense, logical sense and intuition.

The "holds" that a scientist will use and the breadth of his concern will depend greatly upon his subject matter. If one is engaged in an operation comparable to the determination of the atomic weight of zinc, he will use intuition to help him to decide how to proceed; he will use his hands and his eyes in carrying out the operations and mathematical sense in making calculations. He will probably have no occasion in the experiment to use his senses of taste, smell or even hearing. He will be aware that zinc is inanimate and he need not concern himself with the characteristics that are inherent in living things.

If the subject matter of one's investigation is a mouse, he will use all the same equipment used in the experiments with zinc, but in order to experiment intelligently, he will recognize that the mouse not only has the equipment to see, hear and feel, but also a sense of balance, timing, hunger, etc. So far as we know, it will not be necessary to recognize in the mouse any sense of beauty, sense of humor or sense of moral responsibility.

If one is concerned, however, with human biochemistry, the picture changes. The senses used in carrying out investigations will not be so different from those used in experiments with zinc or with mice, but if one is to do a thorough job of investigating, one must take into account all of the attributes and characteristics that are inherent in human beings, and proceed accordingly. Particularly so if one is interested, as I am, with *real* human beings, not with some purely hypothetical creature.

There are some who would regard it as preposterous that a biochemist, as such, could be interested in religion or its possession by any whom he seeks to understand biochemically. However, we have good reason to believe that having a sure-footed religious faith may influence one's internal biochemistry markedly. We know that even such a seemingly innocuous action as placing experimental animals in isolation has strong influences on the working, for example, of their complex endocrine systems.

A scientist who seeks to understand the biochemical workings of human beings cannot know too much about them. If he is going to do the utmost with his mind no holds barred, he will use all the senses that he can muster and he will recognize in his subjects all the characteristics that reside in them. He will be aware of much besides "material things" and will be concerned with much that he cannot see, hear, feel, taste or smell.

We may study the behavior of a rat in a maze, neglecting musical sense, literary sense and all thoughts of religion, without losing any important clues. We cannot hope to understand the behavior of human beings in or out of mazes without taking into account every sense (and every nonsense) they have, and the complex workings of their biochemistry. We cannot hope to understand their biochemistry—fully— without studying them *as they are,* influenced by many things that cannot be seen or heard, like conscience, aspirations and the sense of beauty.

This point of view is not a mere hypothetical or visionary one; it is of the utmost practical importance, for example, in the field of mental health, which concerns all of us. The bridge between psychology and biochemistry is yet largely to be built and it has to be built from both ends; psychology cannot do the whole job; neither can biochemistry. Only as we learn more about how the working of people's minds affects their biochemistry and how biochemistry affects the working of their minds, will we advance surely toward better human understanding and the avoidance of unnecessary mental disease.

There is nothing inherently unscientific about giving consideration to the mathematical sense, the musical sense or the moral sense when we deal with human beings. On the contrary, it is quite unscientific to leave these out. As we look at people and the world around us we may recognize material things—atoms, molecules, aggregates; we recognize ideas as being real and potent; we also recognize that aspirations, ideals and love may greatly influence people's entire lives. Nothing should escape the notice of a scientist (or nonscientist) who wishes to do the utmost with his mind.

CHAPTER XIV

What About God?

The facts of human individuality and many observations that have arisen out of exploring their meaning have contributed much in a constructive way to my ideas about God.

When one affirms that he believes in God, this is relatively meaningless unless at the same time he can give some concept of what the word "God" means to him. This gets into the subject of *theology*.

I should preface anything I say on this subject by making it clear that I regard it as axiomatic that it is wholly beyond human intellectual powers to really understand God. A "worm's-eye view" of God is the best that we can hope for.

This realization should not, however, keep us from doing the utmost with our minds, and we should not fall into the fallacy of assuring ourselves that what we cannot understand does not exist. We have already disclaimed the idea that because we cannot understand how thinking or free will originated on this earth, we should therefore rest assured that thinking and free will do not exist. It is this kind of reasoning, I presume, that causes the fool to say in his heart, "There is no God."

My intuition tells me that just as there are many facets to human minds—psychologists say forty or more—there are probably many facets to God, and that at best we can only gather hints about these various phases.

In attempting to do this, we use our minds the same as when we think of anything else. Some regard religious thinking and faith as belonging in a separate compartment from scientific thinking, but I see no basic difference. In science we make, by intuition, hypotheses and theories in which we have some faith—sometimes too much. In religious thinking we make or consider hypotheses in which we have some *faith* —also, sometimes too much. The difference is in the subject matter of our thinking. In science we make hypotheses and theories about things that can be verified by scientific experiment; in the religious realm our hypotheses and theories concern matters where experimentation, in the scientific sense, may be impotent. Both in scientific and religious thinking we use our minds to answer the questions "In what will I have faith?" and "How much faith?" In both cases no holds are barred.

One aspect of God has already been hinted at in our earlier references to the Divine Plan. From what I know of biology, biochemistry and probability, it appears that what has happened on this earth, and what is happening, could not be if the cards of the universe—the laws which govern it—had not been stacked in such a way as to make it happen within the available time.

It should be clear that I do not pretend to understand how this "stacking" could have taken place, nor do I believe that as scientists we know more than perhaps a small fraction of the basic laws that govern the universe. These laws constitute, in my mind, one aspect of God. God is the orderly laws that make possible the world and all that is in it, including life, thinking, the sense of beauty, free will and moral responsibility.

The universe as revealed by telescopes about fifty years ago was already incomprehensibly large. Light, traveling about eleven million miles a minute, would take tens of thousands of years to traverse it. During the past fifty years, however, astronomical advances have increased our concept of the size of the universe by trillions of times and we have no assurance that the limit has been reached or is near. If we were to reduce the universe of 1915 to a tiny scale model the size of a peanut, and the universe of today were reduced *to the same scale* for comparison, it would be miles across.

It seems highly probable now that there are millions of planets like ours where intelligent beings exist. The realization of this cannot help but modify (enlarge) our concept of God. If we judge the Ruler by the size of His domain, God must be regarded as trillions of times as great as was supposed fifty years ago. The concept of God was then far too big for human beings to swallow and comprehend. It has now become more obvious, if possible, that it is not in the realm of possibility for human intellects to comprehend God. Trying to *prove* or *disprove* the existence of a Being we cannot comprehend intellectually seems like a childish exercise.

Another aspect of God is Beauty. God is, for example, beautiful music. Some individuals have such strong musical sense that this aspect of God is extremely satisfying. Alexander Pope wrote:

> *Some to the church repair,*
> *Not for the doctrine, but the music there.*

A striking example of religious devotion to music is that of Handel, who after months of contemplation went into seclusion at the age of fifty-six, and working for twenty-four days almost as if in a trance, produced the 275 folio pages of the *Messiah*. During this time he had a servant bring some meals to him in his seclusion but he hardly took time to eat or sleep. That such a thing could happen, that what he produced could thrill millions of people for centuries, is an evidence of what I think of as God.

God is also the beauties of nature, beautiful literature, beautiful poetry, beautiful sculpture, beautiful art of all kinds. It is our true enjoyment of these—not a pretended enjoyment to bolster our prestige—that makes us more God-like and less like brutes. If we cannot live without these beautiful things, we cannot live without God.

Another important aspect of God is the love and concern we have for our fellow man. This is extremely widespread. There are, for example, many moderns who may not even care to admit that they have a religion but who nevertheless have a deep concern for humanity. This is an expression of their God-likeness and their fundamental admiration (or love) of God, whether they so designate it or not.

This aspect of God was emphasized by Jesus in the poetic saying: "Inasmuch as ye have done it unto one of the least of these my brethren, ye have done it unto me." Leigh Hunt set forth the same idea in his poem "Abou Ben Adhem" (may his tribe increase) whose name, because he loved his fellow men, "led all the rest" among those whom "love of God has blessed."

Kahlil Gibran in his widely read poetic volume *The Prophet* emphasizes the many-sidedness of religion. The Prophet's extended discourse had been on love, marriage, children, giving, eating, drinking, work, joy, sorrow, and a dozen other diverse subjects when he was asked: "Speak to us of Religion." The Prophet's reply was: "Have I spoken this day of aught else?" ". . . he to whom worshipping is a window to open but also to shut, has not yet visited the house of his soul whose windows are from dawn to dawn."

The facts of individuality have made more reasonable to me an aspect of God which is of great practical importance. There are many who accept the idea of God as a big "IT," the principle which governs the universe. They may even regard Him as the "Master Computer" engaged in a gigantic statistical enterprise who, dealing in a wholesale manner, could not possibly have any concern for or any relations with any individual. Thoughts about individuality and the idea that each individual is highly distinctive, according to the Divine Plan, lead us to take another jump: Perhaps God is far more vast than a big "IT"; possibly He is a "retail" as well as a "wholesale" Operator and is capable of concern not only for the universe as a whole but for *all* the individuals that have evolved under the Plan.

This jump greatly enlarges our concept of God—but should we balk at this? In fifty years of astronomy His domain has appeared to increase trillions of times. It was truly incomprehensible—too large for us to contemplate—fifty years ago; it still retains this quality—expanded in size trillions of times. God is incomprehensible in any case whether His domain is extremely large or is trillions of times larger, and whether or not our concept of Him is expanded to include the idea of His being a retail as well as a wholesale God.

This enlarged concept of God is the essence of Jesus' teaching. He taught that God is a Father who cares individually for his children. Accepting this on authority may be comfortable to some. For me the statement "God is a Father because Jesus said so" is less strong and carries less conviction than if it is put another way: "Jesus said 'God is a

Father'; because it is so." This basic idea of a God great enough to care for individuals rings true to me, taking into account all my intuitions and all I know about the universe and its inhabitants.

The practical importance of this idea lies in the ability of God—if He is that big—to touch each of us individually and be touched by each one of us. This opens up the possibility of our getting, as individuals, help from God. Admittedly we can't see, intellectually, quite how this could be, but let us not for this reason dismiss God–individual relationships as nonexistent.

Perhaps this idea would seem more reasonable if we consider the possibility that God is atomistic and that each of us has a private "atom" of God of our own—like a guardian angel. The number of "atoms" required to give a separate one to every human being who ever lived on a million planets like ours would perhaps be 10^{21}. This is about the number of molecules present in a single drop of water. Maybe God is big enough so he can be atomistic—who knows?

With the playing of the Utopia game, referred to in Chapter IV of this book, there came to me inadvertently considerable light on the question of the prevalence and importance of God–human relationships.

Included in the list of fifty items which the players of this game could choose to take or leave behind was *Religious Worship*. At the time, this item was included simply to make the list as complete as possible; the game was played by science students in a chemistry building; no one had any religious purposes in mind; there were no religious connotations whatever and the game was played anonymously. No one had anything to gain or lose by trying to make religion appear important or unimportant.

This seems—in retrospect—like a fair trial. If these scientifically inclined students thought that religious worship was a meaningless exercise, they would rate it zero; if on the other hand they thought it worthwhile and valuable, they would accordingly give it a higher rating.

The youngsters were uninhibited and showed individuality with respect to this item as they did on all the others—the ratings varied from 0 to 10—but when the tallies were in, *Religious Worship* averaged the highest rating of the fifty items, viz., 7.3; *Marriage* was next with the average score 5.5. When the game was played a year later by a similar group, *Religious Worship* was again at the top with a score of 8 and *Marriage* scored 6. A similar group at another institution played the same game. In this group *Religious Worship* and *Marriage* were tied at the top with a score of 7. In two Negro college groups *Religious Worship* scored at the top 6.4 and 6.7 respectively, while *Marriage* was farther down the list with a score of 3.2 in both cases. When a group of American Indian students in Oklahoma played the game, *Religious Worship* rated the top at 6.0 and *Marriage* rated next at 4.4. Because of a misunderstanding, one time the Utopia game was played the students were asked to sign their names to their ratings. The apparent effect of this on the rating of *Religious Worship* was to make it a little lower than in anonymous groups. There is thus no reason whatever for thinking that students rated *Religious Worship* high in order to impress anyone.

These widespread high ratings indicate that young science students as well as other students often think they have at least a vague contact with God. The striking fact is that they enjoy the experience, whatever it is, so much that they very frequently rate religious worship higher than *anything else,* including athletics, hunting and fishing, eating, flirting, marrying, reading, music, shows of all kinds, driving cars, travel or any other item you care to name. Such a satisfaction-giving item as this must, to them, be very potent and very real.

Religion has always been a matter of greatest interest to human beings. Because of the individuality of people's minds and make-ups they look at the subject in many different ways—this is healthy—but it is striking that they so seldom ignore religion. A few of the great men of history have registered antagonism toward religion—at least the religion of their time—but if they are carefully considered individually, it is found that in most cases the antagonism was directed toward the trappings and window dressings that have been associated with worship; the antagonism was not toward religion or God. Very few of those in recent centuries who are thought of as genuinely great have resisted religion as such; many were *inclined* to believe more than they could give intellectual assent to. Spinoza was a striking example of one who was an independent thinker and could not accept intellectually the common religious dogma. He was abused and called an atheist in his day, but he had strong religious feelings, so strong that in recent years he has even been referred to as a "God-intoxicated man."

The religious sense or the sense of God is deeply imbedded in most of us whether or not we use the same terminology to describe it. If people regarded God as merely a big untouchable "IT" which governs the universe; if they were convinced by experience that nothing is gained by worship; if they had nothing in them that gives them a compelling desire to reach out for God, then churches, synagogues, temples and mosques would be abandoned and we would go our way eating, drinking and being merry—Billy Graham would have no appeal whatever to anyone.

One of the most limited and picayunish ideas that has been generated in our modern age is that God is merely a concept—something that is man-made to meet his imaginary needs. Of course, there are different concepts of God; every individual has a distinctive concept because each of us has a unique mind. Concepts change from time to time and from generation to generation, and this pictures, to those who think of God as merely an image or reflection, an ever-changing God. It is these people presumably who talk seriously about the possibility of God's being dead. They think that if the prevailing mode of thought in our society includes a nonbelief in God, then God is gone. This does not make sense in the light of the facts of individuality. People do not think in concert, and if they could they would not be able to wipe out God. Those who think only in terms of a man-made God believe that there is, as one playwright has put it, really a "vacant bench" on which we are privileged to install, if we wish, a god of our own making. My thought is that *individuals* (who alone can think) may and do have all sorts of ideas about God, but back of their varied and changing concepts lies the Eternal—the Laws of the living universe, Beauty and Love. This Eternal in all its aspects cannot be comprehended by human minds; certainly it cannot be recast, revamped or "killed" by human thinking.

The fact that people are prone to entertain mystical ideas is far-reaching and leads them in curious directions. Strange as it may seem, the wide acceptance of the teachings of Sigmund Freud has rested not a little on people's interest in the unknown and in things that are occult or hidden. Freud emphasized the importance of the "unconscious" and of dreams; if his doctrine had lacked this mystical element, it would probably never have gained acceptance.

Because of the fundamental urge to find God in a mystical sense, a vast host of people hang on tenaciously to religious observances and organizations even when it is clearly obvious that they do not accept the dogmas which accompany them. If religion is dished up to them sprinkled with a flavor they do not like, they try to get the essence and push the objectionable flavor aside. The fact that so many people do this, including ministers, priests and rabbis, as well as many liberal laymen who have perhaps been brought up on fundamentalist ideas, is a powerful testimony to the potency of God and religion in human life, just as is the fact that so many Utopia players, acting with complete spontaneity, rated *Religious Worship* higher than anything else.

The anonymous playing of the Utopia game by sophisticated adults has revealed the fact that while *Religious Worship* is often a strong contender for top rating in these groups, its position on the rating scale is likely to be lower —sometimes far lower—than with the young people for whom the game was originally designed. This probably means that the education we get in our culture tends to swing us away from religious worship. There are two aspects of our education which may do this: one is the emphasis on science; the other is the stress on environmentalism and the accompanying tacit denial of moral responsibility.

There is no escape from the fact that in science just as we do not accept ideas because the "authorities" say so, neither do we accept intuition as providing us with answers to scientific questions. We always wish to submit our intuitions to the test of experiment.

The importance of scientific experiment, however, tends to vanish in some areas of human activity and interest. For example, if I (by intuition) love a certain piece of music— enjoy hearing it over and over—experimentation to determine whether it possesses beauty, such as the statistical analysis of other people's reactions, would have little pertinence to the question of whether it is beautiful to me. Similarly, if millions of people by intuition believe in God and regard religious worship highly, experimentation or analysis cannot be expected to demonstrate one way or the other whether God exists.

To me there is no question whatever but that science can thrive in the hands of those who entertain intuitions and those who have mystical experiences which cannot be subjected to experiment. Science would be crippled only if intuitions and hunches were accepted authoritatively, and if there was refusal to submit these intuitive ideas to experimental verification whenever possible. A scientific education should not blind us to the existence of matters such as idealism, beauty, love and religious worship. These are beyond the confines of any existing science.

Possibly the part of our education which has most effectively tended to lead us away from religious worship is the widespread teaching in current psychology and sociology that our behavior is environmentally determined, and hence that we really have no moral responsibility for what we do. No one can deny that a slum environment, for example, is conducive to illiteracy and crime, but to overemphasize this and to spread the word that all slum dwellers are *ipso facto* innocent and not responsible in any way for their own shortcomings or misdeeds, is not only contrary to the fact that many slum dwellers are good citizens (page 101) but is conducive to the general opinion that whatever *anyone does* can be traced to an environmental cause. This half-truth if taken as the whole truth can undermine all moral responsibility. Some people, it appears, would like to dodge moral responsibility, and an education embodying environmentalistic ideas can furnish this dodge. There are some people presumably who do not want to be "little gods," yet they resent the idea of being puppets. This is one case, however, where people cannot have their cake and eat it too.

Many have, I believe, a false idea of the functions of "religious education." Some think of religion as something to be plastered on young people during their formative years. If they are not gotten to early, they feel, the plastering may not stick. This thought rests, in part, on our environmentalism, and an outcome of this type of thinking would be the conclusion that a child cannot be blamed for his misdeeds if he hasn't been told enough times what is right and what is wrong. This is a dangerous partial truth.

It is my opinion that children have a moral and religious sense that develops quite naturally even if the environment is far from ideal. Individuals with conspicuously high moral sense have appeared repeatedly in history even when their surroundings could not be cited as the cause. Of course a good home is important, yet I resent the idea that religious education is a brainwashing operation. Religious sense needs to be fostered; parents fortunately do not have to create it in their offspring. They could not; it is a part of humanity and of the Divine Plan.

What measures can be taken to make education more constructive and less likely to undermine the deep-seated religious attitudes that children often have? Certainly children cannot be shielded from every concept that might be in conflict with the theology of a passing age. One thing that can be done is to cultivate a poetic sense which will help make students less rigid and formalistic in their thinking.

All students of the Bible, "fundamentalists" and "liberals" alike, agree that the Psalms were meant to be poetry. "The Lord is my shepherd, I shall not want" does not mean —to anyone—that we are actually ruminant sheep or that we will never be hungry even at mealtime. "The firmament showeth His handiwork" does not mean—to anyone—that God really has giant hands—fingers and thumbs—with which He fashioned the heavens. The poetry of the Bible is not by any means limited to the Psalms. We may read in

Genesis: "And God said 'Let there be light' and there was light." Surely no one would take this to mean that God caused His giant vocal cords to vibrate throughout the universe and that as a result the light suddenly came on as though an electric switch had been closed.

When Jesus said, "Blessed are the pure in heart for they shall see God," this was expressing a spiritual truth—the idea that God could be "touched" by those who are pure in heart; it did not suggest that the image of God would actually be thrown on anyone's retina—"No man hath seen God at any time."

I can sympathize with those who are reluctant to admit that the Bible is full of poetry, if, as is too often the case, poetry is thought of as being opposed to truth rather than being a beautiful way of expressing truth. The fact that the Bible is full of poetry does not by any means weaken it. It strengthens it. Extract all the beautiful poetry out of the Bible and it would no longer be a literary masterpiece. It would be a dully written volume which would not be cherished; it would not have survived. The fact that it is full of poetic and figurative language—the interpretation of which is not always simple and direct—allows our individual minds to play upon it and get from it what is good for us, as individuals.

If the idea of poetic expression could be more widely appreciated, students could face the facts of science without being thrown off balance. There are so many valuable ideas that cannot be expressed in mathematical or literal terms; they have to be expressed poetically if at all. When we speak of music "gripping" us, or of God "touching" us or of "holding fast" to our ideals, we are using poetic language. If we use these expressions *literally,* we are misrepresenting the truth, just as the writers of the Bible would be doing if they meant *literally* much that is said in the Bible.

The second thing which can be done to make education fundamentally less disruptive to students' personalities and their capacity to appreciate all that is in life is to *recognize fully their individuality.* Perhaps there is no area in which the need for recognizing individuality is more keen than in the field of religion. The diversity of people's minds is clearly evident even among those who supposedly embrace the same doctrines or belong to the same religious sect. This diversity is as it should be, but it needs to be recognized and taken in stride. We should learn not to fly at each other's throats because we do not see eye to eye. Individual people will, of necessity, have very different ideas about religion.

Among Protestants, for example, there are scores of different sects even though they are supposedly unified by belief in the same Christ and reverence for the same Bible. Among Catholics there is also room for varying beliefs and attitudes. Among its members are those who are nominal members only; in addition, there are six hundred orders in the church. I have been told by a recent visitor to Spain that Jesuits and Dominicans are often so much at outs there that they will not speak to each other. The room for diverse minds within the Catholic Church is one of its strengths.

When the inborn individuality of people is recognized fully, there will be no more search for the *one true interpretation of God* and there will be no cause for distrusting those who do not believe just as we do. When students are taught to appreciate the individuality of their minds, they will be able to choose in the field of religion, without friction, whatever suits them best. Very few, under these conditions, will choose irreligion.

The choice of one's religious beliefs and attitudes is by no means purely a matter of education and bringing up. Children brought up in the same environment do not necessarily agree. Of course, there is some inertia in people, but students in particular should be encouraged to change from the church in which they were brought up, if they want to. The recent switch of Luci Johnson (Nugent) to the Catholic church, where she feels at home, is a compliment to Luci, to the Catholic church and to her father for permitting it to happen without undue stress. I have known individuals who were raised as Catholics who when they gained independence found the atmosphere of that church intolerable and drew away, becoming Protestants. Such transfers—in both directions—have happened in times past. John Henry Newman wrote the famous hymn "Lead, Kindly Light" as an Anglican minister. Later he became a Catholic—even a Cardinal. Shifts such as this should not be rare or accompanied by misapprehension. By encouraging students to be themselves, we will be approaching an age of enlightenment when *education* will not mean *education away from religion*.

My own religious inclinations are such that discussions *about* religion are subordinate to the possession of the real thing—as Jesus conceived it to be—the love of God as a Father and of His children as brothers. I can worship God without attempting to settle all theological problems. This can be done alone or in the presence of those whose tenets may be very different from mine. I have worshiped in many different Protestant churches, including those of the Mormons and Quakers; I have worshiped in Roman Catholic churches, in one Greek Catholic church and in the presence of a devout Mohammedan saying his prayers toward Mecca. In all of these situations I have felt the presence of God. I could doubtless worship in many other groups if I knew more about them and had occasion to. I have not been asked to judge and I do not set myself up to judge to what degree the members of these groups accomplish the purposes of divine worship. I respect their efforts and I suspect that God is able to touch them. Jesus said, "In my Father's house are many mansions."

When I say I *felt* the presence of God, or that God is able to *touch* people, I am, of course, using figurative language. What actually happens cannot be put into words or described to one who has not had a similar experience. "Feeling" the presence of God is akin to the "feeling" one has when he enjoys the beauty of music or literature, or when one has affection for another person. We have not learned yet—perhaps we never will—to put into words many experiences that loom very large in our lives.

The sense of worship is keener at some times than at others; it surely takes different forms in different individuals. Looked at from the standpoint of objective history, it has been a potent force in many millions of human lives.

Religious organizations of all kinds are imperfect instruments for fostering the religious sense. Being *organizations,* they inevitably deal in rules and expect a degree of uniformity on the part of their members. It goes without saying, however, that an organization has the best chance of accomplishing its purposes if its leaders know the characteristics that its members possess. Young organizations are less likely to smother individuality than older ones because their practices have not yet crystallized. Some sort of freshening process needs to be developed so that religious organizations (as well as others) can get away from excessive domination by rules, regulations, precedents and preachments, and from the idea that the function of an organization is accomplished if it successfully perpetuates itself.

Religious organizations need to adapt themselves so that religiously inclined independent thinkers can benefit from them and be benefited by them. It is a striking fact that no church existing at the time could attract to its membership one of the greatest Christians of modern times: Abraham Lincoln. It is by no means certain that any church existing now could attract him. Either they are too full of dogmas that are intellectually unacceptable, or else they are too cold to suit the taste of one who like Lincoln was fervently religious and highly God-conscious.

The ultility of the sense of God, a highly individual matter, is tremendous in that one who gains this sense is never alone, is poised and invulnerable to all attacks. "If God be for me, who can be against me?" One who possesses this sense of God has a peace of mind "that passeth understanding," something to be desired above everything else. "Neither death, nor life, nor angels, nor principalities, nor powers, nor things present, nor things to come, nor height, nor depth, nor any other creature, shall be able to separate us from the love of God . . ."

Not only does the sense of God allow us to keep our sanity in times of trouble and severe stress, but it is possible (although we cannot understand how it can be) to develop a day-to-day working partnership with God and a feeling of oneness with His purposes. We can experience His guiding hand and His readiness to help us in everything we do whether or not it is closely tied to what is commonly thought of as being of a "religious" nature.

This working partnership when in operation frees us from frenetic personal concern and at the same time cultivates in us a deep and abiding desire to be the best and most effective partner we can be. Concern for one's person becomes merged with the desire to forward the Divine Plan. The prospect of having "stars in one's crown" fades into insignificance and death presents no fear if one really feels the presence of God. Our "feverish ways" disappear and the greatest joy in life comes to us. Trust in the Almighty could be absolute and magnificent even in the days of Job:

"Though He slay me, yet will I trust in Him." Whatever the Divine Plan is, a human partner accepts it with the appreciation that God's ways are beyond his full understanding.

Nowadays there are many people, including a substantial number of ministers, priests and rabbis, who have serious doubts about immortality. Certainly there are a host who think that the Biblical pictures of heaven and hell are highly poetic and hence not to be trusted in a definitive or literal sense. These may believe, and many do, that the concept of personal immortality is not only passé but preposterous.

In the light of the facts of individuality and the onward march of science, this question merits another look. In view of the expanded view of God and the universe, the old idea that immortality is "out" because all the millions of souls would be an "indigestible load on the stomach of the Almighty," loses completely its force. We have, in the light of the facts of astronomy, no basis whatever for putting a boundary around God and a limit on what merits His attention. It makes no sense for us to call a halt and say, "God and the universe have expanded well beyond our comprehension already, personal immortality is out." It would be the last straw. This goes back to the fallacy of denying the existence of anything—life, thinking, beauty, God—because we cannot understand its origin.

Our attitude toward this problem may be greatly influenced by our appreciation of science and its development. Scientists in the early 1900's may have imagined that they were well along in the understanding of the physical world of atoms, molecules and energy. We know now, in the light of relativity and many other developments, that scientists of that day were "babes in the wood" and very far from home.

If we believe now that ignorance is on a fast decline

and is disappearing asymptotically, what do we conceive of as the function of science a hundred years from now? Will all the important basic problems be solved? For my part I regard this concept as ridiculous. As we have already indicated, science raises more questions than it answers. We are not approaching the end of the road. Scientists in the early 2000's will probably look back on the scientists of the 1960's with charitable eyes, realizing how limited we were in our outlook. A generation or two later scientists may have the same attitude toward those of the early 2000's.

The laws of the universe are now very incompletely known. Even the various kinds of attractions that exist between atoms and molecules have not been catalogued or described. The biological laws that govern heredity in human beings and other mammals are in a dense fog. Certainly the laws that have made possible the origin of life, thinking, the sense of moral responsibility and of beauty are far removed from the known.

Science in the future will occupy itself in an ever-expanding pursuit. This pursuit will not by any means be exclusively outward toward the planets, stars and galaxies but may emphasize instead the inner space of our minds. Helmholtz, the famous German physicist, hinted at this phase of a widely expanding field of science about a hundred years ago when he said, "Memory, experience, learning are also facts, the laws of which can be investigated." Scientists in the future may be making discoveries in what we now call the "spiritual" realm and they may come to accept as commonplace what we may now be inclined to reject with finality. We are not in our present state of ignorance in a position to say, "Immortality cannot be."

An observation made by the great physicist Arthur Compton seems to point toward immortality. He called attention to the fact that in the realm of physics nothing ever really completely ceases to exist. While electrons, protons, neutrons, mesons (on and on) can undergo certain transformations, they never suddenly or gradually become absolutely *nothing.*

If the Divine Plan was to have life originate on earth and from it to develop, after eons of time, thinking, a sense of beauty, moral sense and a sense of God, then to our human minds, with this sense of God, it seems inscrutable that these most remarkable earthly developments will suffer annihilation, whereas only senseless atoms and molecules and their transformation products last on and on. What about God Himself? He is a Spirit and must be indestructible; what about the "little gods" who are made in His image? Would a fitting epitaph for every human being be: "He rose like a rocket and fell like a stick"? I am idealist enough to think not.

It is true that fear was a factor in the generation of primitive interest in God and the hereafter. Sophisticated minds today may have pretty well banished fear, and while we may have gotten away from the idea that we will strive to be virtuous on earth so that we will be rewarded in heaven, the sense of God remains. Those who possess this sense have a feeling of trust; they do not have their goal set on the next world but they have the confidence expressed in Whittier's stanza:

> *I know not where His islands lift*
> *Their fronded palms in air;*
> *I only know I cannot drift*
> *Beyond His love and care.*

Two desperate needs of humanity stand out: good will and understanding. The cultivation of a sense of God and a partnership with Him will surely foster good will. Understanding is equally essential; people can have good will and yet not be able, for lack of understanding, to extricate themselves from war. Wendell Willkie was right when he said that there exists today throughout the world "a gigantic reservoir of good will" and Winston Churchill was right when he expressed the idea that most people in the world are basically decent and want to live in peace with their neighbors. People cry out for peace but they do not have *understanding* enough to attain it. A basic understanding of people —all peoples—*as they are,* is needed.

Racial and other problems cannot be solved merely by passing laws and enforcing these with bayonets. Changes must take place in people's hearts and in their *minds.* Appreciation of the facts of individuality which we have dealt with in this book is a basic ingredient for the development of peace on earth.

Index

A B O U T   T H E   A U T H O R

ROGER J. WILLIAMS, professor of biochemistry at The University of Texas, was born in India in 1893. He received his B.S. degree from the University of Redlands, his M.S. and Ph.D. degrees from the University of Chicago. From 1940 until 1963 he was director of the Clayton Foundation Biochemical Institute at The University of Texas, where more vitamins and their variants have been discovered than in any other laboratory in the world.

His research led to the discovery, isolation and synthesis of pantothenic acid, an essential cog in the machinery of all living things. He also did pioneer work on folic acid and gave it its name. In recognition of his contributions, Dr. Williams was awarded the Chandler Medal, the Mead-Johnson Award of the American Institute of Nutrition, honorary degrees from Redlands, Columbia and Oregon State and was elected to the National Academy of Sciences in 1946. He was also President of the American Chemical Society in 1957.

Dr. Williams is the author of several textbooks of organic and biochemistry and edited with his colleagues an American Chemical Society monograph on the Biochemistry of the B Vitamins (1950). With E. D. Lansford he edited The Encyclopedia of Biochemistry (1967). Aside from textbooks, his more important writings include: The Human Frontier (1946), Free and Unequal (1953), Biochemical Individuality (1956), Alcoholism: The Nutritional Approach (1959), and Nutrition in a Nutshell (1962).